Other titles in The Knowledge series:

Flaming Olympics
by Michael Coleman

Potty Politics
by Terry Deary

Foul Football
by Michael Coleman

Murderous Maths
by Kjartan Poskitt

The Gobsmacking Galaxy
by Kjartan Poskitt

Awful Art
by Michael Cox

Groovy Movies
by Martin Oliver

The Knowledge

MIND-BLOWING MUSIC

By Michael Cox

Illustrated by Philip Reeve.

Hippo

Scholastic Children's Books,
Euston House, 24 Eversholt Street,
London, NW1 1DB, UK
A division of Scholastic Limited
London ~ New York ~ Toronto ~ Sydney ~ Auckland
Mexico City ~ New Delhi ~ Hong Kong

Published in the UK by Scholastic Ltd, 1997
Text copyright © Michael Cox, 1997
Illustrations copyright © Philip Reeve, 1997

10 digit ISBN 0 590 19570 0
13 digit ISBN 978 0590 19570 6

Typeset by TX Typesetting, Midsomer Norton, Somerset
Printed in the UK by CPI Bookmarque, Croydon, CR0 4TD

23 25 27 29 30 28 26 24 22

The right of Michael Cox and Philip Reeve to be identified
as the authot and illustrator of this work respectively has been
asserted by them in accordance with the Copyright, Designs and
Patents Act, 1988.

Papers used by Scholastic Children's Books and made from wood
grown in sustainable forests.

Contents

Overture   7

A wop-bop-a-teen pop   9

Play it again ... and again ... and again   25

Pop of the toffs?   38

Interval: Ten tuneful terms to test your talents   63

If it moves, play it!   66

The rhythmic roots of some seriously stunning sounds   92

Non-stop pop   116

An A–Z of non-stop pop   154

Michael Cox When he was a little boy, Michael Cox used to play trumpet with top jazz musicians Jelly Roll  Morten and Louis Armstrong. Then his dad took away his record player. Not long after this, his dad also took away his trumpet, so to protect the human race from further harm, Michael decided to become a music *fan* rather than a musician! He loves classical, folk and jazz music, and he's absolutely bonkers about early blues and African pop music.

Philip Reeve Unlovable mop-top Philip Reeve knows nothing about pop music: he can't tell Suede from Slade, and he doesn't know his Radiohead from his  Echobelly. Until he came to illustrate 'Mind-blowing Music', he thought Oasis was a ladies clothes shop, or that green spongy stuff you find in the middle of dried flower arrangements! He's been illustrating books for two years and lives in Brighton.

Overture

Music is invisible. It slips inside people's ears, sneaks around their brains and almost immediately they begin to feel, think, and behave differently. Or to put it another way – music really is **mind-blowing**!

- It can bring tears to the eyes of happy people and make them feel all gooey and slushy inside.

- It can bring smiles to the faces of miserable people and make them jump for joy.

- It can make musicians want to play so perfectly that they practise until their fingers fray ... and their brains become battered blobs of bilge (and that's just the triangle players!)...

- And sometimes it can drive people up the wall...

Lots of people can't live without music. They listen to CDs and tapes, go to concerts, festivals and discos and some of them find music *so* mind-blowing that they even go to the trouble of reading about it in books like this one!

This book will tell you about all sorts of mind-blowing music, the mind-blowing musicians who make it, and the mind-blowing musical instruments they make it with. It will give you all sorts of mind-blowing information about musical instruments which are made from things like armadillos ... bones ... suitcases ... cats...

There's practical advice, too, on how to conduct an orchestra, make your own guitar and become a pop mega-star in just 24 hours.

There isn't space in here to describe every kind of music in the detail it deserves, but hopefully it'll introduce you to some cool tunes that'll really blow your mind.

A Wop-bop-a-teen-pop

During the 1950s a new sort of human being was invented. It wasn't a child and it wasn't a grown-up – it was somewhere in-between and it was called a teenager.

Before this time there hadn't been any teenagers – people had generally gone straight from being children to being grown-ups.

Children hadn't had time to be teenagers before the 1950s because they'd been too busy:

- leaving school at a very early age;
- working really long hours;
- being poor;
- fighting in wars;
- becoming just like their mums and dads;
- and then having their own children.

A few years after World War II had finished, things started to change. Young people (particularly in

America and Europe) suddenly began to get more money than they'd ever had before and lots more time to spend it in. People with things to sell (such as records!) realized that these new-fangled "teenagers" could be their new customers, so they began to make a fuss of them. This made the teenagers feel important and special. When teenagers realized that they were teenagers – and that they were able to make choices about their lifestyles – they got really excited!

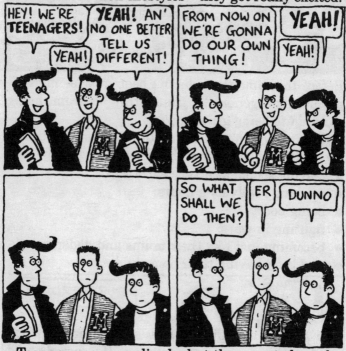

Teenagers soon realized what they wanted – to be different from their mums and dads. They wanted to hang out with their pals and look mean and cool. They wanted their own ridiculous hairstyles (instead of their parents' ridiculous hairstyles), they wanted their own fashions, their own ways of talking, their own dances ... and their own music. Music that was so wild and crazy that it made them want to leap around and scream and shout – they wanted mind-blowing music just like Elvis Presley's ... and Chuck Berry's ... and Little Richard's!

The mind-blowing music star who made your grandma rock, and your granddad roll

When the great rock 'n' roller, Little Richard (b.1935), was 15, he got a job working in Dr Hudson's Travelling Medicine Show. If you don't know what one of these is, just imagine your local Boots the Chemist but with all-singing all-dancing checkout operators ... and a rock and roll band ... and a branch manager who wears a top hat and stands on a stage constantly screaming and yelling at the customers to buy more cough medicine and vitamin pills! Dr Hudson's Travelling Medicine Show sold Miracle Health Tonic (or totally worthless coloured water, as it was known in the trade). During the 1940s it moved very rapidly from one small American town to another (it had to – before people realized they'd been sold a load of rubbish and came asking for their money back!). Little Richard's job was to dance around and scream and sing and shout until a huge crowd assembled to see what all the fuss was about. As soon as lots of people had gathered around, Dr Hudson would cry out something like:

"You lot look absolutely *awful*! I've never seen such a load of unhealthy human beings in my whole life! I bet you'd all like to be full of vim and vigour again, wouldn't you?"

And all the people would wave their walking sticks and rattle their false teeth and Dr Hudson would point to Little Richard and say, "Just imagine what it would be like to be so fit and healthy that you could sing and dance all day long, just like this young groover! He's bursting with good health and energy! And it's all because he drinks lots and lots of my special Snake Oil Health Tonic!"

Little Richard would nod and take a big swig and immediately begin to leap and scream and boogie.

And the crowd would go "Ooow!" and "Wow!" and "Get it on down, man!" and say, "I may be 110, but I sure like to boogie! I'll take a dozen bottles please!" Then they would rush home and drink the tonic and wait for the miracle to take place. After an hour or so they'd feel no different. Eventually the poor things would hobble back to town to ask for their money back but, by this time, Dr Hudson and his show would have upped sticks and hightailed it out of there.

When he was a bit older, Little Richard decided it was time for a career move, so he got a job washing up at a bus station. As he scrubbed the greasy plates he liked to leap around banging on pots and pans and singing things like "Tutti frutti all rootie, tutti frutti all tootie, tutti frutti, a wop-bop-a-loo-mop!"

Not long after this, Little Richard's life was completely changed by Art Rupe (it's not a disease, it's a name – Art was a record company boss. Remember, if you want to get ahead in the music business you've got to have a completely ridiculous

13

name.). Art got Bumps (Bumps Blackwell, the record producer, of course!) to help Little Richard make a record of his washing-up song. It was called "Tutti Frutti" and it sold a million copies! The newly invented teenagers thought Little Richard was absolutely brilliant and they went in their thousands to see his stage shows where he leapt around, screaming and shouting, and playing the piano with his feet (he'd never had proper lessons).

So what had happened? Why do you think Little Richard stopped being a rock and roller? Was it because:

a) he joined the Smurfs?

b) he said he had a message from heaven that told him to stop because God wasn't at all keen on that sort of music?

c) one of the old medicine show customers recognized him at a concert and had him arrested for taking part in a swindle?

It was **b**). This is what happened.

Little Richard had a dream where he saw the world burning and the sky melting and he thought it was some kind of mysterious warning to him. Then he heard that the Russians were launching the Sputnik spacecraft and said that this was a sign that he should maybe stop rocking and rolling.

14

COMRADES — VOT VE'LL DO IS LUNCH ZE FIRST EVER SPICE SHEEP! ZAT VILL PUT A STOP TO ZIS AWFUL AMERICAN ROCKINK AND ROLLINK TYPE MUSIC!

SPOTNIK SPROUT-NIK

SPUTNIK

Not long after this Little Richard was flying to Australia with the rest of his band, when the aircraft began rocking and rolling. Little Richard thought that the engines were on fire so he got down on his knees and prayed to God to save his life. He promised that he would give up rock and roll for ever if he was spared. The plane didn't crash and they all arrived safely. Little Richard was so pleased and grateful to God that he took off all his gold jewellery ($20,000-worth) and threw it into the sea! He then stopped being a rock 'n' roller. He went to Bible school and became the Reverend Richard. He still made records singing Gospel, but some people don't think they're half as good as when he was a screaming, dancing rock'n'roller.

Something to do: rock for idle hands

If the rock 'n' rolling teenagers of the 1950s suddenly got the urge to dance but were unable to do so because they were sitting in a crowded classroom, tube train or public convenience, they did a dance called the Hand Jive. Here's how to do the Hand Jive — you can practise it to almost any of your

15

favourite music but you'll probably find it works better to Little Richard or Chuck Berry than to the theme from EastEnders or the "William Tell" overture by Rossini.

1. Slap both of your hands down on your thighs.
2. Bend your left arm so that your left hand is in the air. Hold your left elbow with your right hand and draw circles in the air with the first finger of your left hand twice.
3. Slap both of your hands down on your thighs.

4. Bend your right arm so that your right hand is in the air. Hold your right elbow in your left hand and draw circles in the air with the first finger of your right hand twice.

5. Hold your hands across your chest, one above the other. Waggle your left hand above your right hand twice – waggle your right hand above your left hand twice.

6. Hold your right hand up as if you are a policeman stopping traffic. Move your hand in a circle as if you are polishing an imaginary window. Do this twice then repeat the action with your left hand.

Well done – you have now got the general idea of the Hand Jive (and bruised thighs).

Important safety and hygiene note. Do not attempt the Hand Jive while you are: a) riding a bike b) hanging from a mountain ledge by your finger-tips or c) eating your dinner.

Ministry of Squares
Extracts from Top Secret Files
Three Extremely Dangerous Guitar Slingers – these men are a menace to respectable music! They must be watched at all times.

Chuck Berry: born 1926, St Louis, Missouri, USA
Real name: Charles Edward Berry
Jobs: rock 'n' roll songwriter, rock 'n' roll performer
Instrument: guitar
Appearance: thin moustache, slim body, large baggy suits, big grin
Description of songs: tell stories, often about ordinary everyday events e.g. car breaking down, catching bus, going to school
Examples of songs: "School Days" (1957) – makes a day at school sound like non-stop fun. "Nadine" (1964) – sees beautiful girl during bus journey. Asks the driver to stop so he can chat her up. "Roll over Beethoven" (1956) – tells classical composers to make way for rock 'n' roll
Distinguishing behaviour: a) Often seen doing "duck walk" (bent knees; body doubled up;

17

grinning; singing; playing guitar; all at same time!) b) tendency to drive teenagers wild.

Buddy Holly: born 1936, Lubbock, Texas, USA
Real name: Charles Hardin Holley
Instrument: guitar
Jobs: rock 'n' roll songwriter, rock 'n' roll performer
Appearance: slim, youthful, large white teeth, large black spectacles
Examples of songs: "That'll be the Day" (1957) and "Peggy Sue" (1957) (said to be "classics" of pop music)
Significant dates: 1959 tragically killed in a plane crash aged 23. **1977** reissue album of hits sold over one million copies in UK alone
Other notable facts: fan paid £30,000 for black spectacles at auction. Style of music and songs much copied e.g. by Beatles, Rolling Stones. Appearance also much copied e.g. by singers Elvis Costello and Jarvis Cocker.

Bill Haley: born 1925, Michigan, USA
Job: rock 'n' roll performer
Instrument: guitar
Appearance: not slim, not youthful, large C-shaped lock of hair stuck to forehead (known as

"kiss" curl!), fondness for wearing tartan suits
Distinguishing behaviour: often lay down to play guitar (obviously extremely lazy!)
Claim to fame: significant song "Rock Around the Clock" (1955) said to have started the rock 'n' roll revolution – it didn't, just brought the music to attention of people who were missing out on it

Rock and roll timeline 1955–62

1955

- Little Richard has million-selling hit with "Tutti Frutti"
- "Rock Around The Clock" massive hit for Bill Haley in USA
- Teenagers go crazy for rock 'n' roll

1956

- Elvis tops US charts with "Heartbreak Hotel"
- Teddy boys riot in UK

1957

- Buddy Holly has hits with "That'll Be The Day" and "Peggy Sue"
- Jerry Lee Lewis has hit with "Great Balls Of Fire"
- Bill Hayley comes to London – teenagers go wild (again!)

1958

- Elvis Presley's "Jailhouse

Rock" goes straight into UK chart at number one – Elvis joins US army for two years

- Madonna born, 16 August, Rochester, Michigan, USA
- Michael Jackson born, 29 August, Gary, Indiana, USA
- New toy craze called "pogo" stick takes off in UK (literally!)

1959

- Buddy Holly killed in plane crash
- Official statistics stated that there were now 500,000 "teenagers" in Britain. According to the same statistics there hadn't been any in 1950 (where on earth had they all come from?)

1960

- Tamla Motown (rhythm 'n' soul) music starts to be popular in USA and the Miracles have hit with "Shop Around"

- Elvis Presley declared public enemy number one in West Germany, after teenage riots

1962

- Cliff Richard has UK top-ten hit with "The Young Ones"
- America and Russia on brink of war over Russian missiles sited in Cuba. World War III almost starts! Superpowers change minds (decide to listen to music instead – phew!)

Shep ... rattle ... and roll

When Elvis Presley (1935–77) was a young man he drove a truck for a living. It wasn't a very well-paid job and Elvis often had to give blood at $10 a pint to make extra money. But he was ambitious and wanted to be a big star.

When he was a little boy he had won a talent contest with a song called "Old Shep". It was a sad ballad about a pet dog that died.

Everyone thought it was a great song but it wasn't really the kind of thing that would get teenagers rocking and rolling in the streets. Elvis needed something else ... music with pzazz! and kerpow! ...

music like the rhythm and blues of Arthur "Big Boy" Crudup (1905–74). Elvis heard Arthur sing a song called "That's alright Mama" and he thought it was brilliant. So Elvis performed the song for a record company. They said, "It's great! Let's make a record of it!" It was Elvis's first hit. He was suddenly on the way to fame and fortune! He began doing concerts and driving his fans wild with songs like "Shake Rattle and Roll" and "Hound Dog". He made more records (including a few more by Arthur Crudup). The teenagers of the 1950s thought they were tremendous and bought them by the bedroom-load.

Rocking ... and rolling in it!

By the time he was 23, Elvis was a multi-millionaire. He was rich enough to buy himself a mansion and he could afford as many Cadillac limousines as he wanted! He even gave new cars to his friends and family as Christmas presents (it must have cost him a fortune in wrapping paper!).

Elvis seemed to enjoy being generous. One day he drove past a man who was mending the fence at his mansion (it was always getting broken by fans trying to get to see him). The man looked admiringly at the brand-new, shiny pick-up truck that Elvis was driving and said:

Elvis made so much money from his records and films that he was able to do almost anything he wanted – including making dreams come true!

Elvis's fans were devoted to him (they still are). One young girl fan once told a newspaper called the *Sunday Graphic* that she could never get ready for bed without first switching off her bedroom lights, because she felt that 2,006 eyes all seemed to be watching her. The eyes belonged to Elvis – the girl had got over one thousand photographs of her hero stuck to her bedroom walls. That's what you call fanatical! When Elvis died on 16 August 1977 his fans rushed to the shops to buy his music. Twenty million Elvis records were sold in one day!

Elvis was particularly inspired by black gospel music and rhythm 'n' blues. He said that black people had been playing this kind of music long before he was born and that it had been generally ignored until he (Elvis) came along and did his version of it. He took Arthur Crudup's black rhythm 'n' blues sound, mixed it with his own country music sound, and ended up with a surefire recipe for success! During his life he broke records as well as making them. He made over 90 long-playing albums which were all hits, and he had over 100 mind-blowing hit singles, 17 of those reaching the number one slot in the UK!

Last verse

Elvis went on to inspire lots of other people, such as the Beatles and Cliff Richard. That's the way it seems to be in music (perhaps in other things as well?). Everyone seems to have their heroes and they strive to be as good or better than them. Their music develops in its own unique and personal way, and then they go on to inspire a new generation of musicians in turn. It's still going on today. Apparently Oasis think the Beatles were a bit of all right – now who was it that inspired the Beatles?

Despite his influence on Elvis, and despite Elvis's generosity to his fans, poor old Arthur "Big Boy" Crudup didn't get a penny for the songs that Elvis turned into hits. Lawyers were still arguing about who should pay what to whom when Arthur died in 1974.

Play it again... and again... and again.

A record achievement

Finding a way to capture sound in a permanent form was one of the hardest technological challenges that human beings have ever faced. It was the sort of problem that could only be solved by someone who had a unique and original approach to things, someone with foresight ... and imagination ... and scientific vision – Thomas Alva Edison (1847–1931).

Thomas started school when he was 8. He stayed for three months, then left never to return. His teachers had decided he was a dimwit. They said his brain was hopelessly "addled" so his mum had to take over his education.

Luckily, Thomas's teachers were completely wrong about him. He turned out to be a creative genius and during his lifetime he thought of (or developed) nearly 1,300 different inventions including the microphone, the electric light bulb and the miraculous sound recording machine that became known as the *phonograph*.

Thomas Edison's sound decision

When Thomas Edison got the brainwave for his phonograph ("sound writer") machine he asked one of his assistants, John Kreusi, to make it for him, then he recorded his own voice on it. This is what happened next:

25

Thomas and his helpers were so thrilled and amazed by this miraculous new invention that they stayed up all night playing with it and singing into it and hearing their own voices played back. It was brilliant fun! They were making the first-ever recorded sounds! Perhaps it had the potential to catch on? Even Thomas Edison was astounded by his amazing machine. A bit later on he said,

I was never so taken aback in my life!

Thomas quickly realized that his invention was going to affect the lives of millions of people for ever, and he made a list of all the possible uses the machine might be put to. One of the things he said was:

THE PHONOGRAPH WILL UNDOUBTEDLY BE LIBERALLY DEVOTED TO RECORDED MUSIC

YOU CAN SAY THAT AGAIN!

THE PHONOGRAPH WILL UNDOUBTEDLY BE LIBERALLY DEVOTED TO RECORDED MUSIC...

In 1879 the first-ever advertisement for a phonograph appeared in a magazine. Which magazine do you think it was?

a) the *New Musical Express*

b) the *Pony Express*

c) the *Boys' Own* paper

d) the *Radio Times*

It was **c**). Why? Well, at that point, whoever was marketing the phonograph thought of it as more of a "toy" than an incredibly useful and world-beating invention that would eventually change people's listening habits for all time.

Your favourite superstars in your own living room

Thomas was right about the phonograph being used for pleasure – in no time at all people had rushed out to buy their very own sound machines and were soon using them for their personal entertainment. The idea of being able to listen to their favourite stars over and over again in the privacy of their homes was a totally novel and thrilling innovation for the pop-pickers of the late 19th century.

Other people weren't quite so thrilled with the new invention. The British composer, Sir Arthur Sullivan (1842–1900), didn't think it was a very good idea at all. He said,

I am terrified that so much hideous and bad music may be put on record forever.

27

For the record

The phonograph was just the start of many fantastic inventions that have helped to bring all that terrible music right into our living rooms. This is what happened next:

- 1877: Thomas Edison invented his phonograph.
- 1878: the Edison "Parlor Speaking Phonograph" went on sale for the first time.
- 1888: the first-ever flat gramophone record was introduced in America by Emile Berliner.
- 1892: master discs were developed so that lots of copies could be made from one original recording. Records were now made from rubber.
- 1895: rubber discs were replaced by ones made of shellac – shellac is a sort of resin made by insects (so perhaps these were the first ever Beetles records?).
- 1905: a record company called Stollwerk began making records out of chocolate!

- 1925: the microphone was developed (and singers were finally given something to do with their hands!). The first electrically recorded discs were produced.
- 1948: long-playing records were introduced. Shellac records were replaced with plastic ones (**Weird fact** – During the 1950s there was a craze

28

for making things from plastic records. Creative teenagers would soften their unwanted plastic singles in very hot water and turn them into attractive and useful household items such as plant pots, fruit bowls, clock faces... [**Warning**: you will not be able to do this with your unwanted Michael Jackson and Take That CDs even though they are made from plastic.])

THINGS YOU CAN DO WITH YOUR OLD C.D.S

A NICE SAUCER

STABILISER WHEELS FOR YOUR BIKE

THIS LOVELY HAT

- 1952: Britain's first singles chart was published in the *New Musical Express* (NME). The number one record was "Here in my Heart" by Al Martino.
- 1958: stereo records (where the sound appears to come from different directions) sold for first time in Britain and America.
- 1963: compact cassettes go on sale for the first time in the UK.
- 1968: manufacturers go "two better" than stereo and invent "quadraphonic" sound – four speakers, one in each corner of the room, intended to give a "surround sound" concert-hall feel to listening. Doesn't really catch on.
- 1979: first Sony Walkman goes on sale.

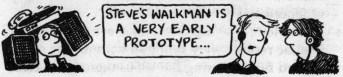

STEVE'S WALKMAN IS A VERY EARLY PROTOTYPE...

29

- 1983: compact discs (CDs) sold for the first time in Britain and the USA.
- 1995: Toshiba Company of Japan reveals plans for launch of "video CD" player (as an alternative to video tape). Video discs can contain up to seven hours of music.
- 2000 onwards: well ... what do you think? Hi-fi sound that is actually more "realistic" than the real thing? Instruments that play themselves in the style of your choosing at the flick of a switch? Maybe even all-singing, all-dancing holograms of your favourite bands performing just for you, in the comfort of your own living room or bedroom?

The competition goes flat out

In the years that followed Edison's invention, another inventor called Emile Berliner (1851–1929), decided to improve on Thomas's original design by

30

replacing the wax cylinders with flat discs. In order to play the flat discs Emile invented a machine called a gramophone. For a few years the gramophone and the phonograph were in competition, but eventually the public decided that they preferred gramophones – the sound quality was much clearer (but still incredibly scratchy and indistinct compared to modern CDs). By the early 1900s, discs had virtually taken over from cylinders. Just think! If they hadn't done you might now be going to things called end-of-term cylinderothèques and dancing to music coming out of CC players (work that one out for yourself!).

By gum ... that sounds good!

It's surprising that Emile's gramophones became so popular, especially as the owners of the first ones were advised to listen to their records through their teeth! This is (more or less) what the instructions told them to do:

How to get the most (vibrations) out of your Gramophone:

Congratulations! You are the proud owner of a "Gramophone". It should bring you hours and hours of listening pleasure. After many months of patient research here at the "Gramophone" company, we have discovered that the best way to listen to the gramophone is not through your ears ... but through your teeth! So here's what you will need:

a) a stick, smallish (walking sticks, hockey sticks, etc. are not suitable)

b) a darning needle (i.e. the kind used to mend socks)

c) two large wads of cotton wool

And here's what to do:

1. Attach the darning needle to the stick.
2. Stuff the cotton wool in your ears.
3. Hold the stick between your teeth.
4. Fit the tip of the needle into the outer groove at the edge of the disc.
5. Wind the gramophone so that your disc revolves at exactly 70 revolutions per minute.
6. Dig those groovy sounds, they should feel like music to your ... teeth?

When they were finally able to buy gramophones with loud speakers and wind-up springs, most music fans must have been overjoyed. Years later, things got even better ... they were provided with electricity to make their discs go round!

Sing it again ... and again ... and again

Despite all the initial "teething" troubles associated with the new-fangled gramophone record players, musicaholics were obviously as pleased as punch at being able to listen to their favourite sounds over and over again and quite soon gramophone discs

32

began to sell in their thousands. The stars themselves may not always have been entirely happy
about the new technology (even though they were
probably making lots of money out of the records).
Mass production of discs hadn't been invented in the
19th century so this meant that instead of just doing
one "take" and then going home to put their feet up,
the musicians had to repeat their performances
over, and over and over again. In other words, one
performance for each record (or each ten records, if
a batch of ten recording machines was used simul-
taneously).

In 1892 a record "pressing" process was developed.
The recording technicians "cut" one master copy of a
performance at a recording session. From this
original, thousands of copies could be mass-
produced or duplicated ("pressed") in a factory – a
bit like the way newspapers, books and magazines
are produced on a printing press.

Ah Pooch'ini ... my favourite!

In 1899, a British artist called Francis Barraud
(1856–1924) recorded his voice on to a wax cylinder.
He then played the recording to his pet dog, whose
name was Nipper. The record was an instant hit
with the little dog.

SIT! SIT! SIT!

I AM! I AM! I AM!

As little Nipper wagged his tail to the ace sounds that were coming from the phonograph, Francis painted a picture of him. When the painting was finished he called it "His Master's Voice". Francis showed "His Master's Voice" to a company that made gramophones and records and it gave them an idea. They said that if he replaced the phonograph with a gramophone they would use the picture to advertise their discs and record players. Francis made the alteration and this picture began to appear in shop windows all over Europe.

The advertisements were a huge success (...and in no time at all, dogs everywhere were rushing out to buy their very first gramophones). The picture of little Nipper eventually became so well-known and liked by members of the public that the company decided to rename themselves after the original painting. They changed their name from the "Gramophone Company" to "His Master's Voice". You are more likely to know them as HMV.

Jukebox heaven (or hell?)

In 1906 someone came up with the idea of putting coin-operated music machines in public places, so that people could choose their favourite discs and pay to listen to them whenever they felt like it.

These machines (which were really a sort of musical robot) actually replaced live musicians in many places of entertainment. They were called jukeboxes – after the small bars and cafés in America where people gathered to listen and dance to live music and generally have a good time. Not everyone was keen on the jukebox – especially the real live musicians who lost their jobs. Also, having to listen to other people's favourite records played over and over again can be very, very annoying.

Silence is Golden

When the CBS record company realized that some people were annoyed by jukebox music they came up with an idea to give them some temporary relief from unwanted sounds. What do you think they did?

a) left little bowls of free earplugs on the tables in the bars and cafés that had jukeboxes?

b) made a totally silent record that could be included in the jukebox selection?

c) had lots of sets of headphones linked to the jukebox so the listeners could enjoy their favourite music without upsetting other customers?

It was **b**). In 1952, the CBS company issued a record called "Three Minutes of Silence". It goes like this...

Tranquil, isn't it?

Silent record enthusiasts would probably enjoy the work of the modern composer, John Cage (1912–1992). In 1952, John composed a piece of piano music called 4'33". It consists of one note of music (so that the audience know it's started) followed by four minutes and 33 seconds of total silence, during which the audience are supposed to imagine whatever music they feel like hearing...

Last note

Thomas Edison's sound recording machine was a great idea that definitely changed everyone's life for the better. And, of course, if it was suddenly "disinvented" we would all be lost without it ... wouldn't we?

What do you think?

Pop of the toffs?

Not *all* music is created with the intention of making people jump, jive and boogie all night long. Some music is intended to be listened to more thoughtfully and quietly well, that's what a lot of people think about classical music, but are they right?

Let's clarify matters (and save further trouble!) by having a look at a couple of definitions:

Classical music: strict definition as used by music students, musicologists, etc.

Music of an orderly nature with qualities of clarity and balance and emphasizing formal beauty rather than emotional expression.

The classical period was (roughly from 1750–1830) a time when other arts like architecture, design and painting were reflecting the classical styles of ancient Greece and Rome. Great emphasis was placed on the careful construction of neat, elegant and well-balanced compositions in both classical music and architecture. Examples of composers from the classical period are Haydn, Mozart and Beethoven.

Classical music: not so strict (loose) definition as used by music superstores, radio stations, the public in general and this book.

> *All music that* isn't *pop, rock, folk, country and western, jazz, blues etc. Examples of composers: Satie, Stravinsky, Grainger, Puccini.*

And now that's sorted out we can move on to...

The young idiot's guide to some different types of classical music

Orchestral music: Music that is written to be performed by large groups of musicians and instruments known as orchestras. Music lovers often go to concert halls to listen to orchestras – sometimes with over 80 instrumentalists – performing things like symphonies and concertos (...and to have a really good cough!).

Chamber Music: Chamber music groups usually contain from three to eight players. One of the most important sorts of chamber groups is a string quartet – made up of two violins, one viola and one cello (plus four musicians to play them of course). This sort of music was originally written to be performed in a small room (or chamber). So, if you see a group of musicians performing chamber music in the middle of a field, report them immediately!

Opera: An opera is a play in which the words are sung to music. Opera originated in Italy at the beginning of the 17th century. If you want to know what it feels like to take part in an opera, why not try singing your way through a whole day? With the help of your friends and family you can turn otherwise boring conversations into stirring solos (single singing sections) and rousing choruses (group singing sections). Try this for starters:

Symphony: A piece of music which is intended to be played by an orchestra. It is usually divided up into three or four sections (or "movements"). Symphony concerts often last for quite a long time (so always take sandwiches and a change of socks).

Concerto: A piece of music that is written to feature a solo instrumentalist being accompanied by the rest of the orchestra. The soloist obviously gets the lion's share of the musical action while the other instrumentalists contribute at the appropriate moments (...or check their lottery numbers and take short naps).

Sonata: A piece of music written for a small group of musicians or a solo performer accompanied by one other instrument. The accompanying instrument is often a piano – unless the piece happens to be a piano sonata.

Oratorio: A Bible story set to music for solo voices, chorus and orchestra. It is not like an opera because the performers do not act.

Got that? Good! You're now ready to attend a concert of classical music, but remember – you must be on your best behaviour! Everyone knows that the sort of people who listen to classical music are extremely respectable and well-behaved. None of them would ever dream of carrying on like wild rock and rollers or those outrageous punk rockers ... would they?

Eric Satie and the Pinheads

The French composer, Eric Satie (1866–1925), wrote the music for a ballet called *Parade*. In order to give his ballet a really modern sound, Eric decided to add some trendy new instruments to the orchestra like a few typewriters ... and some whistles ... and a pistol! When Eric's new work was performed in Paris in 1917, his futuristic sounds didn't go down too well. The clattering and whistling and explosions seemed to get on the nerves of certain people in the audience and they began to boo and hiss and shout out rude comments. They were not a happy bunch of music lovers.

In those days it was the fashion for women to decorate their heads with enormous hats and – in order to stop them falling off when they were running for the bus – they always held them securely in place with enormous pins. This turned out to be rather unfortunate for Eric and his pals. By the time

41

the ballet had finished many members of the audience were seething with rage and desperate to let Eric know what they thought of his weird music. The furious women pulled the pins from their hats, leapt from their seats and rushed at the stage in a kind of mini-bayonet charge. They obviously thought that Eric and the other musicians were in need of a few short sharp shocks!

EEK! OWCH! OW!... HEY-THAT GIVES ME A GREAT IDEA FOR A SONG!

How well would you cope as an orchestral musician?

Composers and conductors use the Italian language to instruct musicians how to play. So pick up your fiddle and pay attention! What would a conductor mean if he or she yelled:

1. Pizzicato!
  a) Make your instruments sound like a cat having a tiddle?
  b) Hooray, the pizza delivery man is here?
  c) Pluck the strings of your instruments with your fingers rather than playing with the bow

2. Diminuendo!
  a) Stop staring out of the window?
  b) Gradually play your instruments more and more quietly?
  c) Gradually play your instruments more and more loudly?

3. Lento!
    a) Play slowly?
    b) Wake up Len, this means you too!?
    c) Play swiftly?

4. Largo!
    a) Everyone sing "La la laar!"?
    b) Play in a slow and stately manner?
    c) Play lots of really big notes?

5. Tutti!
    a) Whole orchestra play this bit?
    b) Everyone play this bit in the style of Little Richard?
    c) Everyone toot!?

6. Arco!
    a) Listen to me?
    b) String players use your bows?
    c) Everyone wave their instruments in the air!?

7. Con brio!
    a) Play with more spirit?
    b) Play with more spit?
    c) Get your pens out and take notes?

8. Legato!

   a) Let's all play smoothly?
   b) Let's all play snappily?
   c) Let's all play snap?

Answers: 1c, 2b, 3a, 4b, 5a, 6b, 7a, 8a

Three Mind-blowing Record-breakers – Followed by a Fusillade of Flops!

Fans of classical music aren't the dreary spirits or "stuffed shirts" that people sometimes think they are. They are just as full of passion and enthusiasm about their music as any posse of popsters. They certainly aren't reluctant to show their appreciation if they've enjoyed a piece of mind-blowing music. Sometimes, when they've experienced an extra good performance, the applause goes on … and on … and on…

- At the end of a performance of Verdi's *Otello* in Vienna in 1991, the audience thought that Placido Domingo (b. 1941) had sung brilliantly. They started to applaud the star of the Italian opera, and continued to clap for another hour and twenty minutes.

- The record for the most curtain calls ever taken is held by the opera singer Luciano Pavarotti (b. 1935). He actually took 165 of them after a

1988. The audience didn't do too badly either. They managed to keep clapping for a total of one hour and seven minutes!

I HOPE THEY STOP APPLAUDING SOON... I'M DYING FOR ME SPAGHETTI HOOPS!

- When audiences have particularly enjoyed a performance, they often ask for an "encore" (a repeat of a solo or some extra music). In 1792, the Austro-Hungarian emperor, Leopold II, was so knocked out by a performance of an opera by Cimarosa (1749–1801) that he asked the performers to do an encore of the whole opera! Refusing the requests of all-powerful and hard-hearted people like emperors can be bad for your health so it was a case of "Play it again, Cim!"

- Other audiences at concerts of classical music have occasionally been so affected by musicians' performances that they've given them lots of pats on the back ... cow pats, that is! During the 19th century, concert-goers in the country areas of southern Europe went to performances armed with assorted farmyard manure, just in case the show wasn't up to scratch.

In Paris in 1913, one particular piece of music really got up the noses of classical music fans. The Russian composer, Igor Stravinsky (1882–1971), had written the music for a ballet called the *Rite of Spring* in which a young girl is made to dance herself to death as a sacrificial offering to the god of Spring. The first-night audience had gone along expecting to see a rather pretty and charming ballet about the joys of spring (bunny rabbits, daffodils ... that sort of thing), so they were a bit surprised when they saw scantily dressed dancers "springing" saucily around the set to the shocking and savage strains of Stravinsky's score – and they reacted rather angrily. They didn't just throw rotten fruit, or boo or hiss, or rip up their programmes, or make raspberry noises (which was what they usually did when they were displeased) – they decided to have an all-out riot!

WAM – the nob's favourite!
The ruling classes of 18th century Europe didn't riot or throw cow pats when the Austrian composer, Wolfgang Amadeus Mozart (1756–91), performed his music – they gasped and said things like:

What lovely music! Mozart is sensational! Oh, if only he'd come and give a performance at my chateau – I'd be so chuffed!

That was the way it was in those days, classical music wasn't going to be performed for large public audiences until the next century. Instead it was performed in private at the homes of the rich and powerful nobles. The very richest families kept groups of musicians on permanent stand-by in their palaces and mansions so they could have musical entertainment whenever they felt like it – much like most people now have their own sound systems at home – but with slightly more realistic sound quality!

SO WHAT DO YOU THINK OF MY NEW STEREO SYSTEM?

47

Mozart wanted to appeal to ordinary folk. He tried to give his music an unpretentious, earthy feel, because he wanted it to appeal directly to people's emotions – he once referred to this directness and honesty in his work by saying that he wrote his music, "as sow's piddle"! Some of Mozart's operas became the "pop" music of their day.

WAM's European mega-tour 1763–66

During the 1760s, Mozart went on the road and did a round-Europe mega-tour during which he visited places like:

He gave concerts to the aristocratic families of the day and his audiences included princes, queens and emperors. The toffs went bananas over him! Here are some of the things that happened when the great musical genius was on tour – which are true and which are false?

1. Mozart was invited to visit the palace of the Austrian Emperor, Francis I, so that he could entertain the monarch and his friends. During the visit the great musician slipped on a highly

polished floor and landed on his bottom. The emperor's daughter, Marie Antoinette, picked him up, set him back on his feet, gave him a big hug and kissed him better. Mozart immediately kissed her back and said, "You are very kind, I will marry you!" True/False

2. While Mozart was on the British leg of his mega-tour he visited the Tower of London. In those days it was traditional to keep a few lions at the Tower. When the lions saw Mozart they roared ferociously and the great genius immediately became very frightened and somewhat tearful. True/False

3. When he wasn't performing his music in front of huge, appreciative audiences of rich people, Mozart liked to make his own entertainment. One of his favourite ways of relaxing and leaving behind the pressures of being an international mega-star was to put a stick between his legs and pretend that it was a horse. He would then have fun galloping around the room, clicking his tongue and making giddy-up noises... True/False

Answers: They're all true! Why? Because Mozart was only *seven* when he began his mega-tour of Europe! He was what we call a *child prodigy* – that's someone who doesn't see the point in waiting to grow up before they become brilliant at what they do, so they start almost immediately.

SEND ME AMADEUS BABY!

WIG OUT WILD CHILD!

GET ON DOWN, YOU FUNKY LITTLE 18TH CENTURY PHENOMENON!

WAM the child who drove 'em wild!
Record of achievement:

Age 3: Learned to play the clavier (a sort of piano) brilliantly.

Age 5: Could read and write music and was composing his own concertos.

Age 7: Had mastered the violin — played it beautifully at concerts (no dying cat noises)

Age 12: Had composed and conducted first opera and written over 80 other compositions, including Masses, symphonies and arias — now world famous

- The composer, Joseph Haydn (1732–1809), once said to Mozart's dad: "Before God and as an honest man, I tell you that your son is the greatest composer known to me!" Another composer, Anton Dvorák (1841–1904), said "Mozart is sunshine!"

- Mozart died when he was only 36 years old (...so deciding to start his career at such an early age actually turned out to have been a really smart move!). If he hadn't got cracking so quickly he would almost certainly have never found the time to write:
- 20 operas and operettas* (*little operas)
- 41 symphonies
- 27 piano concertos
- 23 string quartets* (*music for four stringed instruments)
- 40 violin sonatas
  ...and much, much more magnificent music!

There's only one Ludwig Van Beethoven!

One of Mozart's admirers was the German composer, Ludwig van Beethoven (1770–1827). Mozart thought that young Ludwig had the makings of a career in music. He said that he would, "make a noise in the world before long." He was right! Beethoven spent all of his life making and composing great music ... and breaking the rules on the way.

The composer with attitude – Beethoven's music: key notes

- His best-known work is his 5th Symphony. You may know it. It's the one that begins... "Da, da, da ... daaa! Da, da, da ... daaa!"
- The British writer, E.M. Forster (1879–1970),

51

described the 5th Symphony as "the most sublime noise that has ever penetrated the ear of man'.

- The American pop singer Billy Joel (b.1949) said of the 5th Symphony: "It's fate knocking at the door. It's one of the biggest hits in history. There's no video to it, he didn't need one!"

- Although Beethoven composed in the "classical style" that was prevalent in the late 18th century, his approach was much less formal and far more dramatic than that of the composers who had preceded him. He broke quite a few of the rules that they had all stuck to quite strictly – as a result, his music is packed full of passion and overflowing with feeling.

- If you listen to the 5th Symphony and enjoy a good earful of its dramatic changes from soft to loud passages, its rapid switches from slow to fast playing, its soaring solos, crashing crescendos, triumphant trumpets, heart-stopping horns and (occasionally) vicious violins – you'll be able to understand why German playwright, Bertolt Brecht (1898–1956), said Beethoven's music "always reminds one of paintings of battles."

- Modern European politicians obviously recognize the uplifting effects of Beethoven's music – the "Ode To Joy" from his 9th Symphony has been chosen as the anthem of the European Community (so stand up now … **and sing it!**).

- Listen to the storm movement in his "Pastoral" Symphony (number 6) with its thundering drums and seriously stroppy strings and before you know it you'll be hiding under the table … or desperately searching for your wellies and umbrella!

- Listen to the second movement and you'll be wondering if you left a window open as you hear the clarinet sounding just like a cuckoo, a flute trilling like a nightingale and the oboe calling like a quail.
- This tendency to be less formal in his composition and to create dramatic sound pictures that bring to mind the beauty and moods of nature led to Beethoven's music, like Chopin (1810–1849), Liszt (1811–1886) and Brahms (1833–1897) being described as "Romantic" ... as opposed to "Classical" in its strictest sense!
- Beethoven was a composer with lots of "attitude" – both in life and music. He didn't like the old system where musicians (like Mozart) had had to rely on the rich and powerful aristocrats of Europe to support their musical career – he wanted to be independent and make his own way in the world. On the whole he wasn't all that impressed with the ruling classes. He thought more of people who created their own success and wealth, rather than just inheriting it.

YOU ARE A PRINCE BECAUSE YOU WERE BORN A PRINCE – I AM A GREAT MUSICIAN BECAUSE I HAVE STRUGGLED AND STRIVED AND WORKED MY SOCKS OFF ALL MY LIFE! THERE ARE LOTS OF PRINCES... THERE IS ONLY **ONE** LUDWIG VAN BEETHOVEN!

He had a point, didn't he?

What does make composers and performers like Mozart and Beethoven great? Where do they get their phenomenal talents from? If you wanted to become a genius of classical music how would you go about it? Well, you've definitely got to make an early start! There's be no point in waiting until you're 32 if you are planning on becoming a child prodigy like Mozart. It might even be a good idea to start before you're born... your mum might come in useful here – especially if she's anything like Percy Grainger's mum.

The Mrs R. Grainger method for turning children into superstars

Quite a few people think that the Australian musician, Percy Grainger (1882–1961) was a genius. "What an artist, what a man!" – that's what another famous musician, Edward Grieg (1843–1907), said about Percy.

Percy was a brilliant pianist, a world-famous composer, a collector of folk songs and an inventor of music-making machines. One of his best-known arrangements is called "English Country Gardens" – a version of it was a UK pop chart hit in 1962.

Mrs Grainger was determined young Percy would grow up to be exceptionally talented:

1. When she was pregnant she took a Greek statue to bed with her in the afternoon and stared at it as she began to doze off, thinking about things like art, beauty and creativity.

2. When Percy was a boy she made him stay indoors (away from other boys) and read, study music, draw pictures of hens ... and copy his father's collection of nude paintings!

3. She made him practise the piano for at least two hours a day, and if he was ever naughty, she whipped him with a horse whip!

By the time Percy was ten he'd given 12 successful concerts and he was considered by everyone to be a child phenomenon (similar to a child prodigy but harder to pronounce).

"Soothing Savage Breast"

Percy grew up to be quite an eccentric and hyperactive character but a lot of his compositions are gentle, uplifting and very sensitively written. The English playwright and poet, William Congreve (1670–1729) said that music "hath charms to soothe a savage breast, to soften rocks, or bend an ancient oak."

William was right, music works wonders – a pleasant sound can turn raging maniacs into purring pussy cats in second... The power that music has to affect moods, can even save your life, as the composer, Alessandro Stradella (1638-82) found out.

THE KILLERS TURNED UP AT A PERFORMANCE OF ALESSANDRO'S LATEST MUSIC, THE ORATORIO GIOVANNI SAN BATTISTA. THEY PLANNED TO FOLLOW HIM HOME AFTERWARDS AND CARRY OUT THEIR WICKED DEED...

AS THEY STOOD AROUND WAITING FOR THE CONCERT TO END THEY BECAME MORE AND MORE MOVED BY THE MUSIC...

BY THE END OF THE PERFORMANCE THEY WERE SO OVERCOME WITH EMOTION THAT THEY COULDN'T BRING THEMSELVES TO DO AWAY WITH THE MAN WHO CREATED SUCH GORGEOUS SOUNDS

THEY IMMEDIATELY CONFESSED THEIR EVIL PLAN TO ALESSANDRO AND ADVISED HIM TO HIDE AWAY SO THAT NO HARM WOULD EVER COME TO HIM

A "down-beat" tale of death!

That was a nice story, wasn't it? Now here's a sad one! Music not only saves lives, it causes deaths...

PARIS INFORMER 1687
LULLY LAID LOW!

We are sorry to report the tragic death of the Italian composer, Jean-Baptiste Lully (born 1632). Monsieur Lully was a real all-round musician and bright spark. During his career he was a strolling player, a ballet dancer, a violinist, a string band leader, a composer of ballet music and other music. He eventually rose to become personal director of music to our esteemed King Louis XIV. Monsieur Lully was conducting a piece of music which he'd written in celebration of the king's recovery from a serious illness. As the music played he used a big stick to beat time. Unfortunately, as he tapped away, he accidentally bashed himself on the foot with the stick. The blister that came up afterwards went septic and he eventually died from his wound. He will be most sorely missed.

Baton regardless

When Jean-Baptiste Lully bashed himself with his stick he was engaged in the musical activity known as conducting. You may have seen conductors strutting their stuff on the television or at a concert. Some people think their job looks easy – but it isn't! It's demanding and exhausting – some conductors lose weight during a performance. One of the conductor's main tasks is to make sure that the members of the orchestra all work together in order to create a harmonious and unified sound.

Something to do: conduct your own orchestra

Here's how to have power and influence over as many musicians as you can shake a stick at. You will need:

a) a symphony orchestra. These are sometimes booked up months in advance. If you can't get one, don't be disappointed, just use a CD or tape player.

b) a CD or tape of some orchestral music e.g. Mozart's Symphony number 25, Beethoven's "Pastoral" Symphony.

c) a conducting stick – this is your baton. Any of the following will do: a blunt pencil, a banana, a carrot, stick of rhubarb or celery, but avoid anything too sharp.

d) a podium (optional). This is the little platform that conductors stand on. If you've not got one, are under one-and-a-half metres tall and want the musicians to see more than just your hands … you'll have to stand on a chair.

e) smart clothes. A white bow tie and a tail coat would be perfect but failing that your school uniform, Junior Nurse or Spiderman outfit will do. It is essential that you command the respect of your audience and musicians (or CD player).

What to do:

1. Use your *right* hand to hold your baton and control the speed (tempo) that the music is played at. The actions you make will depend on the "time signature" of your chosen piece of music. Here are three to be going on with:

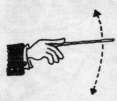

Two beats to the bar: in other words, the music goes *one*, two, *one*, two. This is known as "March Time" (because it's good for marching to). The baton action is a straightforward up and down movement like this ...

Three beats to the bar: like this *one*, two, three, *one*, two, three. This is sometimes known as "Waltz Time" (because it's good for waltzing to). For this one you must make three movements in a triangular shape: one down, one to the right, and one back up again. Be very careful not to get the baton stuck up your nose on the last one!

Four beats to the bar: One, two, *three*, four, *one*, two, *three*, four. For this one you have to make a cross-shaped movement. One down, one to the left, one to the right, and one up (...now unravel your arm!)

Remember, one of the most important jobs of the conductor is to make sure that the whole orchestra keeps perfect time – so no matter what happens don't ever lose your tempo during a performance (but by all means have a good tantrum afterwards!).

2. You use your *left* hand to beckon or "cue in" different musicians when it is their turn to play. Also use your left hand to "shush" musicians when you want them to be quiet. If you have longer than average arms take care not to punch the first violinist in the teeth or knock off the viola player's specs as they will be sitting directly in front of you.

3. Use *both hands* to make big gestures like this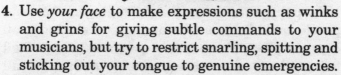

4. Use *your face* to make expressions such as winks and grins for giving subtle commands to your musicians, but try to restrict snarling, spitting and sticking out your tongue to genuine emergencies.

5. Use your *whole body* to leap wildly around, but make sure you don't fall off your podium. Somersaults, cartwheels and headstands are best avoided during quiet passages.

61

Last verse: Music that isn't Pop ... but is Popular!

In 1990, an aria (solo) from a Puccini opera was chosen by the BBC as their theme tune for the World Cup football tournament. The aria, which was from the opera Turandot, was called "Nessun Dorma" and it was sung by Luciano Pavarotti. The whole piece gradually builds to a spine-tingling climax and the great man positively singing his lungs out ... just the thing to accompany a slow-motion replay of a last-minute goal heroically scored in injury time!

When the single was released the song got to the UK top three position in the top 20 singles chart and people could be heard humming and singing it all over the place. Thousands of pop fans (and football fans), who had previously known nothing at all about opera, discovered Puccini's music for the first time and became hooked on it. Perhaps some people feel a bit afraid of classical music. Perhaps it takes a "Nessun Dorma" to make them realize what they're missing?

Interval: Ten tuneful terms to test your talents

Test your knowledge of the language of music by selecting the correct definition for the following words (or see if you can guess):

1. **Note**
   a) A written instruction left out for the milkman.
   b) One individual musical sound.
   c) An awkward tangle, often found in violin strings or shoelaces.

2. **Harmony**
   a) Hair conditioner.
   b) The sound made when two or more musical notes fit together.
   c) French humming music.

3. **Chord**
   a) A trouser material popular with musicians and arty types.
   b) Two or more notes played at the same time that usually sound quite good together.
   c) A singing part for a group of vocalists.

4. **Stave**
   a) The five lines on which

musical notes are written.
b) The name of the busker who plays outside the bus station.
c) A small stick that conductors wave at orchestras.

5. **Bar**
   a) A place where musicians wet their whistles.
   b) A group of musical beats marked out by vertical lines in written music.
   c) A small stick that conductors wave at orchestras.

6. **Melody**
   a) A sequence (or string) of notes that make a pleasant tune.
   b) How musicians used to address aristocratic women.
   c) 1970s female pop singer.

7. **Tone**
   a) Stave's best mate.
   b) The kind of sound produced by an instrument which makes it sound different from other instruments.
   c) Another word for a melody.

64

8. Pitch

a) A place where celebrity musicians hold charity concerts and football matches.

b) A juicy fruit with large stone.

c) The highness or lowness of a musical note.

d) The spot outside bus station where Stave stands.

9. Clef

a) The oldest pop singer in the world.

b) What musicians throw themselves over if they hit a wrong note.

c) A sign placed at the beginning of a stave indicating the pitch of the music written after it.

GOODBYE CRUEL WORLD!

10. Polyphony

a) A musical imitation of a parrot.

b) A parrot that has learned to use the phone.

c) A style of music using two or more melodies at the same time.

ALLO?

Answers: 1b, 2b, 3b, 4a, 5b, 6a, 7b, 8c, 9c, 10c

If it moves, play it!

The piano that Mozart played his music on moved in more ways than one. Mozart's fingers moved the keys, the keys moved the "hammers" of the piano, the hammers hit the strings, and the strings moved the air around them. The vibrations of the moving air then caused the eardrums of the audience to vibrate. The brains of the listeners turned those vibrations into "sounds". The audience found the sounds that they heard very moving... Music definitely seems to be all about movement of some sort or another, and musicians have a tremendous choice of instruments to play all this moving music on ... especially if they've got plenty of money to spend...

Sounds Expensive

The Millionaire's Musical Instrument Superstore!
HERE'S A SELECTION FROM OUR FABULOUS RANGE OF INSTRUMENTS

CREATE TOONS TO SWOON TO WITH THIS SUPERB STRADIVARIUS VIOLIN

♪ LOVINGLY CREATED JUST FOR YOU BY **ANTONIO STRADIVARI** (1644-1737) THE MASTER INSTRUMENT MAKER WHO MADE AT LEAST 1116 INSTRUMENTS DURING HIS CAREER, INCLUDING 540 VIOLINS, 12 VIOLAS AND 50 CELLOS

♪ RENOWNED FOR THAT SPECIAL "STRAD" SOUND. (THE SECRET'S IN THE VARNISH, YOU KNOW!)

♪ AND THE GREAT THING IS IT SOUNDS BETTER THE OLDER IT GETS!

♪ IF YOU'VE GOT ANY SPARE CHANGE WHY NOT COMPLETE THE SET WITH THIS STRADIVARIUS CELLO, PURCHASED AT **SOTHEBY'S AUCTION HOUSE** ON 22ND JUNE 1988 — SIMPLY A SCOOP AT £682,000

♪ THIS EXCELLENT EXAMPLE OF STRADIVARI'S WORK WAS PURCHASED AT **CHRISTIE'S AUCTION HOUSE** ON NOV. 21ST 1990 - AN ABSOLUTE SNIP AT £902,000

EVERY ROCK MUSICIAN'S DREAM – A FABULOUS FENDER STRATOCASTER GUITAR

☆ MADE BY THE FAMOUS **FENDER MUSICAL INSTRUMENT COMPANY** OF CALIFORNIA.

SPECIAL FINANCE DEAL– NO STRINGS ATTACHED!

☆ THIS ONE BELONGED TO **JIMI HENDRIX.** HE USED IT AT THE FABLED **WOODSTOCK FESTIVAL** IN THE U.S.A. IN 1969

☆ A REAL STEAL AT JUST **£198,000**

A STUNNING STEINWAY GRAND PIANO

𝄞 SUPERB RICH AND POWERFUL PLAYING
TONE... RESPONSIVE KEYBOARD...
USED BY TOP CONCERT PIANISTS
ALL OVER THE WORLD!

𝄞 THIS SPLENDID EXAMPLE WAS DECORATED
BY THE ARTISTS LAWRENCE ALMA-TADEMA
AND EDWARD POYNTER IN THE 1890'S

𝄞 IT WAS PURCHASED AT **SOTHEBY PARKE
BURNET'S AUCTION HOUSE** IN NEW YORK.
A GIVE-AWAY AT £163,500

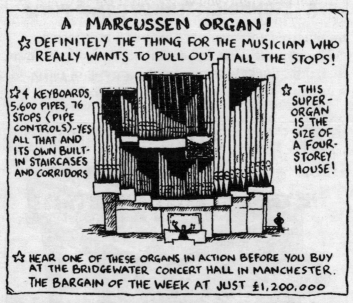

A MARCUSSEN ORGAN!

☆ DEFINITELY THE THING FOR THE MUSICIAN WHO REALLY WANTS TO PULL OUT ALL THE STOPS!

☆ 4 KEYBOARDS, 5,600 PIPES, 76 STOPS (PIPE CONTROLS)-YES ALL THAT AND ITS OWN BUILT-IN STAIRCASES AND CORRIDORS

☆ THIS SUPER-ORGAN IS THE SIZE OF A FOUR-STOREY HOUSE!

☆ HEAR ONE OF THESE ORGANS IN ACTION BEFORE YOU BUY AT THE BRIDGEWATER CONCERT HALL IN MANCHESTER. THE BARGAIN OF THE WEEK AT JUST £1,200,000

The musical instrument we were all given for our 0th Birthday

Confronted with a musical monster like the Marcussen organ, some musicians might change their minds about pulling out all the stops and decide that they'd be happier with a much smaller model after all. If they did, they could always choose the economy-size organ that we all have ready fitted … the one that's called the larynx or voice box.

Your larynx is situated about halfway down your neck. Put your fingers on it and sing something. *"Somethiiiing!"* Did you feel the vibrations? They were caused by two muscles situated in your voice box called your "vocal cords". They sort of "shivered" or "twanged" as a column of air from your lungs (windbags to you!) passed across them.

If you're a child, you've got vocal cords which are about eight millimetres long. Women's are about 11 millimetres and men's are about 15 millimetres.

These miraculous, low-maintenance built-in voice instruments can sometimes earn professional musicians an absolute fortune.

THE SAN FRANCISCO SNOOPER

1882 〜〜〜●〜〜〜 **10 DIMES**

THEY'RE JUST BATTY ABOUT PATTI!

Some crazy people will go to the most ridiculous lengths to hear the noises that come from other people's voice boxes! As I type this piece, I can see a queue of music fans outside our famous San Francisco Opera House (and my front door!). This queue of music freaks stretches the length of four streets and they've been there for almost a whole month now…

Who's in the queue? Well I'll tell you, it's a bunch of opera nuts and they're all waiting to see Adelina Patti, the dame they call the best soprano singer in the world.

Adelina Patti (1843–1919) key notes

- Adelina knew that her fortune lay in her larynx and she took really good care of it. To ensure that it was always in tip-top form she never drank tea, coffee, red wine or spirits and never ate any

71

bread, sweets or cold food.

- Her efforts were well worth the while. She was paid £1,000 for *each* performance she gave (don't forget, this was the 19th century. In those days that kind of money would buy you a Rolls Royce and still leave you change for a mountain bike).

- When Adelina gave her sparkling farewell concert she was wearing £200,000 worth of diamonds. As this was obviously something of a security risk she insisted on being accompanied by two police detectives throughout the whole of her performance.

- With the proceeds from her performances, Adelina bought herself a modest 34-bedroomed Welsh castle to live in. It also had a private theatre, a ballroom with a hydraulically operated floor and, of course, a squad of 40 servants to look after her and her precious larynx.

In 1905, when Adelina was over 60 years old, she was persuaded to make her first-ever gramophone record. When it was played back to her, she heard the sound of her own voice for the first time in her life ... and she just couldn't believe her ears! What happened next?

a) She burst into tears and said, "What a horrible racket ... if I'd known I sounded that bad I'd never have taken up singing in the first place!"

b) She couldn't understand where her voice was coming from so she put her head inside the loud speaker horn of the gramophone to investigate. She became completely stuck and the fire brigade had to be called to rescue her.

c) She began blowing kisses at the record player and said, "Ah, my love! Now I understand why I am Patti. Oh yes! What a voice! What an artist!"

It was **c**). When the record was played back to her she immediately became her own most devoted fan – modest wasn't she? Actually, she was genuinely amazed at the sound of her own singing.

OOH, I'M BRILLIANT! I MUST RUSH OUT AND BUY ALL MY RECORDS!

Something to do

If you've not heard it before, why not record the sound of your own singing voice on a cassette tape player – most modern ones have a built-in microphone and an easy to operate recording device, maybe even a karaoke facility. Stand at the appropriate distance from the microphone (30 centimetres ... 60 centimetres ... 15 kilometres?) and sing your favourite song into it. You may well be surprised (or appalled) by the way your voice sounds. If your tape recorder is of a reasonable quality the sound you hear will definitely be more like the way other people hear you rather than the way you "think" you sound.

How did it go? Was it **a**) a pleasant thrill or **b**) did it make you violently ill? If it was:

a) You are now obviously completely delighted with the results of your recording experiment, just like Adelina, and may already be looking forward to a long and successful singing career.

b) Oh dear! You are now so devastated by the atrocious and unearthly sounds you've just heard that you've probably already sworn a vow of lifelong silence and may even now be on the way to your local monastery. But there's no need to despair, after all, you could always become a station announcer ... or make a good living out of your horrendous singing voice.

Half man – half trumpet?
The 1930s American singing group, the Mills

74

Brothers, didn't yell or screech, they just sang beautifully and played some brilliant musical tricks with their vocal chords. They were so skilful that people listening to their records were convinced that their singing was being accompanied by a trumpet, a double bass and lots of other instruments. The listeners were completely fooled – the only real instrument that was being played on the records was a guitar... The other instruments were all brilliant imitations that the talented Mills Brothers cleverly conjured up out of their versatile voice boxes!

Drumming home the message!

The Mills Brothers used their voices to imitate instruments. Other musicians use their instruments to imitate voices. In Nigeria, West African drummers are able to imitate the speech patterns of their local Yoruba language and can send messages to people up to 30 kilometres away, using what are known as "talking drums".

The drum messages are based on voice patterns of changing rhythms and pitches, and have been used in Nigerian society for hundreds of years. The different pitches are produced by using strings to tighten or slacken the skins on the drumheads as they are being beaten. The tighter the skins, the higher the sound.

SO... HOW DOES YOUR DRUMMER GET YOU TO TALK?

BEATS ME...

Name that Instrument

Despite the fact that they give their instruments a regular thrashing, African drummers treat their drums with great reverence and respect. Western musicians also have a great deal of regard and affection for their instruments – they even go as far as giving some instruments nicknames. Seven of these nicknames are included in the following concert review. See if you can you match each name with the correct instrument?

BOY, WHAT A BAND THAT WAS! THE GUY ON THE **LIQUORICE STICK** (1) WAS REALLY HOT TO TROT! AND THE GIRL ON THE **SQUEEZE BOX** (2) NEVER LOST HER GRIP ON THINGS FOR ONE MOMENT. THE **AXE** (3) MAN MATCHED THE **BONE** (4) MERCHANT'S MEATY SOLOS WITH SOME RAZOR SHARP RIFFS. FOR A FINALE THE **FIDDLE** (5) PLAYER DID A GREAT DUET WITH THE GIRL ON **MOUTH HARP** (6) AND OF COURSE THE WHOLE THING WAS BACKED BY SOME WICKED **TRAP** (7) WORK!

a) trombone **b)** clarinet **c)** harmonica **d)** violin **e)** accordion **f)** drums **g)** guitar

Answers 1b 2e 3g 4a 5d 6c 7f

The malady lingers on

Even though musicians do occasionally give pet names to their chosen instruments, they sometimes find them a complete pain in the neck ... and the mouth ... and the thumb. Constant practising for up to four hours a day followed by long symphony concert performances can lead to all sorts of painful afflictions, like:

"Fiddler's neck": a painful red patch on neck. Violinists get this as a result of constantly pressing their instrument into their neck just under their jaw.

"Glissando thumb": swollen thumb. This problem is caused by instrumentalists regularly sliding their thumbs across the keys or strings of pianos or harps in order to create a rapidly changing succession of notes.

"Emphysema": swollen lungs. This is an unpleasant lung condition that players of brass instruments such as trumpets and trombones get from regular puffing and blowing.

"Clarinetist's lip": puffy and bloody lip. This arises from the pressure of the mouthpiece of the clarinet on the player's lower lip. So remember, if you see someone in the street with their bottom lip sticking out  they aren't sulking ... they're a clarinet player!

Having read this you probably won't want to become a musician. Why not become a professional rugby player or a policewoman, it might be safer?! Or you might like to try a different sort of instrument.

Bottom of the pops

When a clarinetist plays a wrong note on his instrument he refers to it as having played, a "bum note". Musicians do not like playing "bum" notes – that is, unless they happen to be someone like the Frenchman, Joseph Pujol(1857–1945). In Joseph's case, his fans all thought his "bum" notes were the tops!

Joseph Pujol – the man with the musical posterior

YES – ZAT IS RIGHT STAVE. WHEN I WURZ A LEETLE BOY I GOT UNE BIG SURPRISE...

...I DISCOVERED ZAT I 'AD ZE **MUSICAL BOTTURM!**

QUELLE 'ORREUR!

YOU WERE SITTING ON A FORTUNE!

ZAT IS CURRECT. OF COURSE, I KNEW ZAT I WAS GOING TO 'AVE TO START AT ZE BOTTOM AND WORK MA WAY URP...

ZE MORE I TRIED, ZE MORE I GOT BEHIND IN MA WORK!

IT'S TRUE LISTENERS! HIS BOTTOM BECAME MORE AND MORE VERSATILE! NOT ONLY COULD IT PLAY TUNES, IT COULD DO IMITATIONS OF THE VIOLIN, THE DOUBLE BASS. AND THE TROMBONE!

IT WAS AS IF I 'AD A WHOLE ORCHESTRA TUCKED DOWN MA TROUSERS! SOUSANDS OF PIPPLE CAME TO SEE ME. I BECAME MORE POPULAIR ZAN ZE GREAT ACTORS AN' SINGERS OF MA DAY. MA AUDIENCES LOVED ME – ZEY THOUGHT MA PERFORMANCES WERE A HOOT!

ONE OF JOSEPH'S MOST FAMOUS TRICKS WAS TO PLAY THE FLUTE WITH HIS BOTTOM. HE ATTACHED THE FLUTE TO HIS BACKSIDE WITH A RUBBER TUBE AND TOOTLED AWAY TO HIS HEART'S CONTENT! HE'S NOW GOING TO GIVE US AN EXCLUSIVE RADIO 1 PERFORMANCE OF THIS TRICK. WHAT ARE YOU GOING TO PLAY FOR US, JOSEPH?

I WOULD LIKE TO PLAY "BLOWIN' IN ZE WIND"!

Pet sounds

Throughout history, lots of animals have all unenthusiastically donated some of their most intimate and essential bits and pieces in the cause of great music. Thanks animals!

The South American stringed instrument known as a "charango" was once made from the hard outer skin of armadillos (sort of tortoises with attitude). The practice of making charangos out of armadillos was banned after the Bolivian government decided that it was cruel and inhuman. Charangos are now made out of wood. The armadillos are much happier … although short-sighted ones do occasionally ask charangos for a date.

The body of the Japanese string instrument known as the shamisen is made from the skin of a cat. Some people think this gives the instrument a purrfect tone – others may think it sounds just like a … skinned cat?

And to make your didgeridoo, didgeridon't! Just get some "assistants" to didgeridoo it for you!

Rather than being made into instruments themselves, some animals prefer to do the making. When the aborigines of Australia want a new didgeridoo (long pipe instrument), they cut a long straight branch from a eucalyptus tree and bury it in their local white ant (termite) mound. As the amazingly helpful and industrious termites do not wish to antagonize the aborigines, they immediately get busy, nibbling out the centre of the branch.

After a few weeks the didgeridoo is ready! Everyone is happy! The ants have had a fabulous nosh up and the aborigines have a new musical instrument. All they have to do now is decorate it and play tunes on it.

Something to didgeridoo

You can make your own didgeridoo from a hollow cardboard tube – the longer the better – or some plastic plumbing pipe (or why not recycle the family vacuum cleaner?).

To play the didgeridoo, hold it over one half of your mouth and make raspberry noises into it. Add variety and excitement to your didgeridoodling by occasionally making authentic Australian animal noises ... the snarl of an ant ... roar of a termite ... that kind of thing...

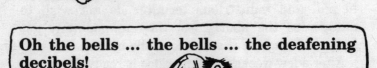

← BLOW IN HERE

MUSIC EMERGES HERE

Oh the bells ... the bells ... the deafening decibels!

The loudness of musical instruments (and other sounds) is measured in things called decibels – the louder something is the more decibels it gets. To give you an idea of the way this works, here are some examples of the sort of sounds we all hear every day along with some musical sounds and their measurements in decibels:

	MOUSE HUMMING	**2 DECIBELS**
WHERE DO YOU THINK YOU'RE GOING? OUT! JUST OUT!	TWO MICE HAVING A REALLY BIG ARGUMENT	**7 DECIBELS**
	HUMAN WHISPER	**20 DECIBELS**
NURP! (SCUSE ME)	ELEPHANT BURPING (POLITELY)	**40 DECIBELS**
	TWO PEOPLE HAVING A CONVERSATION	**50 DECIBELS**
	SAXOPHONE BEING PLAYED BY JAZZ MUSICIAN	**70 DECIBELS**
?	SAXOPHONE BEING PLAYED BY AN ELEPHANT	**0 DECIBELS**
	PAINFULLY LOUD ROCK CONCERT	**150 DECIBELS** (120 DECIBELS IS THE LEVEL AT WHICH MUSIC IS SAID TO BECOME PAINFUL...SO TURN YOUR CD PLAYER DOWN **NOW!!**)

Guitar Monster

Someone who made masses of delightful (deafening) decibels of sound come out of his amplified electric guitar was Jimi Hendrix. Many people think that Jimi was one of the greatest rock guitarists ever and quite a few '90s bands have been influenced by his imaginative and exciting playing. Although Jimi became famous in the late 1960s he started his musical career in the 1950s playing in the bands of rock 'n' rollers such as Little Richard. Little Richard actually sacked Jimi because he refused to wear the uniform that the rock 'n' roller liked the rest of his backing group to wear (so that his own shimmering suits and sparkling shirts would be even *more* noticeable!).

Jimi was generally a bit of a rebel (like Little Richard really!) and at times he seemed to go out of his way to make life difficult for himself. Although he was actually left-handed, he insisted on playing a right-handed guitar. In order to do this he had to play the instrument upside down. As Jimi drove his fans wild with his long "improvised" solos he would perform all sorts of spectacular tricks – holding his guitar behind his head as he played it, or playing it with his teeth. Jimi loved his guitars so much that he wrote poems on the back of them to let them know just how much he cared about them.

Later on, just to make sure that they knew he really, really loved them he would smash them to pieces during his concerts! He obviously felt very sorry afterwards because he usually attempted to stick the broken guitars back together again.

In 1991 the remains of one of Jimi's broken guitars (one with a poem written on it) was sold for £30,000 at an auction of pop bits and pieces.

I'VE BOUGHT HIS GUITAR - I'VE BEEN FOR LESSONS - I'VE READ THE BOOKS - I'VE WATCHED THE VIDEOS - AND I STILL CAN'T PLAY GUITAR LIKE JIMI HENDRIX!

TWANG TWANG. TWOINK

Make your own guitar and learn to play it like a rock mega-star in just seconds!

First a few remarkably simple technical notes on the way an acoustic guitar (and lots of other stringed instruments for that matter) works.

- The guitar is a sort of sound box with strings.
- Nylon or metal strings of different thicknesses are stretched across its body.

- When the strings are picked or plucked they vibrate. The sound produced is amplified as it bounces around inside the hollow box of the guitar's body and finally escapes through a hole.
- The different thicknesses of the strings produce a variety of vibrations which are heard as individual musical notes.
- The thin strings produce *high* notes like *eeeeekk!*
- The thick strings produce *low* notes like *flumpth*.
- The guitarist can add to the variety of notes which are produced by lengthening or shortening the strings. This is done by pressing the strings against the fingerboard with the fingers of one hand while the other does the plucking.
- These two different hand activities are quite difficult to do at the same time – a bit like patting your head and rubbing your tummy.

To make a guitar Jimi Hendrix might have been proud of you will need: a sharp knife and an adult to help you do some tricky cutting, masking tape, a cardboard box (a fruit juice carton will do), a small piece of thickish card, some elastic bands of varying thicknesses, a large helping of imagination (essential).

1. Take your box and make sure there are no holes in it. If there are, cover them up with masking tape.
2. Got all the little gaps and holes covered? Good, now cut

a hole in your box. This hole is going to be the one that the crucial sounds will eventually escape through.

3. Make a bridge. Cut out a piece of the thickish card and score it. Now fold it into a triangular shape and stick it with tape. Cut six small notches in the bridge (one for each string to rest in). Securely glue the bridge to the box just below the sound hole. The bridge will raise the strings away from the guitar's body.

4. Now stretch the various sized elastic bands around the body of your guitar and over your bridge. Start with the thinnest on one side and work across to the thickest. You can have more, or fewer, than six strings if you want – some of the very earliest guitars had only one string.

5. You can now decorate your guitar – or even write a poem on it. It's got to look good as well as sound good!

That's that then. You are now the proud owner of a very sophisticated piece of musical hardware. Just imagine the stunned reaction you'll get from thousands of music fans when you walk on to the stage at Wembley Arena carrying this little beauty!

You can now pluck away to your heart's content. Listen to the different "notes" the strings produce. Try pressing on the strings to shorten them as you pluck them and listen to the way this changes the pitch of the notes.

A suitable case for treatment

Your elastic band guitar was home-made or improvised, it wasn't bought from a shop or a professional instrument maker. Someone else who used improvised instruments was the American jazz musician, Josh Billings. Josh made his own drum from a suitcase! He covered the case in crinkled, brown wrapping paper and stroked kitchen brush whisks over it in order to make a really nice, "Kerrrcherr, kerchherr, cherrrr!" sound. When he wanted a "Clud, clud, kerthunk, thud" kind of sound, he would give the suitcase a few hefty kicks with his heel.

88

Josh was in a jazz band called the Blue Blowers. The Blowers often played at parties held by rich people. The wealthy guests thought Josh's drumming was brilliant and they would show their appreciation of his skills by dropping five dollar tips on top of his suitcase drum. They would be astonished to see the money instantly disappear from sight – as if by magic! Without missing a beat in his drumming performance, clever Josh would neatly flick the money off the case and catch it under his armpit!

DIY drumkits aren't just something invented by eccentric jazz musicians. People have been improvising instruments ever since music began.

- The "pans" (drums) of Caribbean steel bands are made from empty oil drums which are carefully hammered into shape until they sound just the right notes.

- The well-known percussionist, Evelyn Glennie, has a collection of over 700 percussion instruments but she still performs on pots and pans as well. She has had a piece of music written for her to perform on kitchen utensils. It is called "My Dream Kitchen".

Something to do: Improvise a drumkit and play a paradiddle!

What you need: old suitcases and empty containers such as boxes, yoghurt and ice-cream tubs for drums; wooden spoons, pencils or rulers for drumsticks.

What to do:

1. Experiment to discover the different sounds you can get from your "kit".
2. Select your two favourite drums and put one at your right hand and one at your left.
3. Take your sticks and beat the drums as follows (L=left hand R=right hand) L R L L R L R R L R L L R L R R...

In the world of percussion this technique is known as a "paradiddle". It's what drummers do when they're practising. Start fairly slowly then work up to a rapid beat as you gain confidence. Once you're feeling really confident why not try doing a double or triple paradiddle, or even tossing your spinning sticks into the air and then catching them again without missing a beat...

Finale

It's amazing that Josh Billings should have been able to make such hot and "kicking" sounds from something as simple as a suitcase. Perhaps you don't have to spend a fortune on an instrument to be able to turn in a successful performance (or just have some fun?). Perhaps the most important thing about an instrument is that it should be capable of producing the sort of sounds that may actually "move" the listener in some way or other. The sounds may move them to tears, they may move them to laughter, they may move them to move (dance), they may move them to want take up an instrument themselves, if they're produced by an unmusical next-door neighbour they may even make them want to move house (but let's hope not).

The rhythmic roots of some seriously stunning sounds

A really horrible story

Place: Senegal, West Africa
Time: early 18th century

The inhabitants of a small village are just settling down for the evening. They're laughing and joking and generally feel as though they haven't a care in the world. But they couldn't be more wrong!

Under cover of darkness, a gang of strangers has surrounded their settlement. Suddenly the strangers attack and brutally drag the villagers from their homes. In no time at all, the terrified inhabitants are roped together, quaking with fear. Some of them are beaten ... or even killed ... for daring to resist their attackers! They are then forced to march hundreds of exhausting miles to the coast. On the way, anyone who stumbles or cannot keep pace is whipped mercilessly.

When the villagers arrive at the seashore their clothes are stripped from them, their heads are shaved and they are forced into cages. A ship arrives and the captain and his thuggish henchmen come ashore and begin to examine the helpless villagers as if they were cattle at market. He strikes a bargain with the gang leader and money changes hands. The villagers have been sold! They are now herded aboard the ship and jammed below deck as tightly as sardines in a tin. The heat is almost unbearable, the stench is sickening – there are already hundreds of other prisoners down there, the men and boys are chained, it is dark and there is an atmosphere of gloom and misery. The timbers of the ship start to creak and a voice cries "Up anchor!"

Cold terror strikes into the souls of the villagers as they realize that the ship is setting sail. They now know, deep in their hearts, that they will never return home – nothing in their lives will ever be the same again!

That was a sad and terrifying story and unfortunately, for large numbers of people, it was also a true one. Between the 17th and 19th centuries, millions of men, women and children from Africa were taken prisoner just like this and shipped to America to be cruelly used as slaves by the owners of huge cotton and tobacco plantations.

"But what's it got to do with music?" you may ask...

Well, quite a lot actually if we're talking about the stacks and stacks of seriously stunning sounds that fill at least two-thirds of most music mega-stores. Believe it or not, when those ruthless slave traders were so heartlessly transporting the captive African people towards a future of misery and hardship in America, they were also accidentally, helping to create the beginning of much of the popular music we listen to today.

To put it simply, if the terrible trade in human beings *hadn't* taken place pop music as we know it *just wouldn't exist*! For starters ... there would be no:

ROCK, RAP, ROCK'N'ROLL, RHYTHM'N'BLUES, ROCKABILLY, REGGAE, RAGGA, ACID JAZZ, TRADITIONAL JAZZ, MODERN JAZZ, JUNGLE, GOSPEL, CALYPSO, ZYDECO, BLUES, DANCE, HEAVY METAL, PUNK, HOUSE HIP HOP, TECHNO, SOUL

Nor would there be any:

Oasis, Blur, Michael Jackson, Madonna, Tina Turner, De La Soul, Beatles, Elvis Presley, Louis Armstrong ... not to mention a few thousand other stars, groups and types of music that have been enjoyed by hundreds of millions of people around the world over the last 80 years or so. It doesn't leave much in the popular section does it? This is what happened...

Nothing but their Music

When the slave traders dragged their prisoners aboard their boats they didn't ask them if they'd perhaps like to bring a toothbrush or a fresh change of underwear! The African people could only take with them what was in their heads, in other words, memories of their homes, their families, their daily life and ... the thing that was (and still is) incredibly important to people all over Africa, *their music*!

94

WELCOME TO AMERICA: THE LAND OF GOLDEN OPPORTUNITY
(WELL ... FOR SOME ANYWAY!)

The slaves weren't the only large group of people who travelled to America. Between the 17th and the 20th centuries, immigrants from Britain, France, Italy, Spain, Scandinavia, Russia and Germany also made the long and dangerous sea crossing to the "New World" (as Europeans called it) for many different reasons. They also took their music with them. The main difference between these newcomers and the  African ones was that the Europeans weren't in chains – they *chose* to go to the New World!

The musical cooking pot

As a result of the arrival of so many people from so many different backgrounds, America became a sort of enormous musical cooking pot (it still is in many places). Bubbling away inside the pot was a stew made up from a mind-blowing menu of musical flavours and ingredients.

95

THE GREAT AMERICAN MUSICAL STEW

MAIN INGREDIENTS: African music including work songs from West Africa, Senegalese dance music; Yoruban tribal chants; drum music and lots, lots more...
European music including English church and folk music; Spanish flamenco music, European classical music, French and German brass band music plus much, much more...

METHOD of PREPARATION: Mix together well and simmer gently for at least 200 years, stirring occasionally. Should be ready to serve somewhere around the beginning of the 20th century.

SERVING ADVICE: Take care when sampling: much of the music that finally comes out of this pot will be absolutely red hot! Should provide enough exciting musical nourishment (and ideas for future musical meals) to keep half the world satisfied for at least 100 years to come!

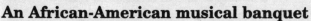

An African-American musical banquet

At the beginning of the 20th century the incredible musical cooking pot boiled over – as the record industry was beginning to take off ... that was lucky! Stacks of sizzling new sounds suddenly set millions of toes and fingers tapping and popping throughout the United States of America. Much of

this fresh and exciting new music was made by
the descendants of the African slaves, (African
Americans as they are sometimes called).

**Seven scintillating black American sound
sensations that set the United States
shimmying and shaking:**
The country blues Mournful, rhythmic, haunting
singing and playing of instruments. Songs were
frequently about sad subjects, musicians made up
(improvised) their own songs and accompanied
themselves on guitar (and sometimes harmonica) –
they often used the "slide" technique where bottle
neck or knife blade is slid up and down strings as
they are plucked.

Jug, skiffle or spasm band music Part blues, part jazz music, very lively, full of fun and energy, not in the least bit slick or polished. Made by black Americans mainly between 1900s and 1940s in places like Memphis, Tennessee, using home-made instruments such as a) washboards (originally used for scrubbing clothes) scraped by musicians wearing thimbles b) old stone whisky jugs – musicians blew across neck opening of these to make a deep rhythmic buzzing sound c) kazoos – cigar-shaped metal instruments that make the same sound as blowing a comb wrapped in tissue paper d) bones and spoons to make a pulsating rattle and clatter.

Boogie-woogie Thumping, rhythmic exciting piano (sometimes guitar) playing that originated in very rowdy clubs. The left hand of the pianist pounds out repeated musical phrases while the right hand plays more complicated and intricate tune. The driving, powerful style of boogie-woogie developed because the places where it was played were very noisy and the pianists had to make themselves heard without microphones or amplifiers. Pianists sometimes put metal tacks in the hammers of the piano, and newspapers behind the strings to make them sound even louder.

Jazz In 1865, after the end of the American Civil War, slavery was abolished altogether. Many freed slaves moved from cotton plantations to towns and cities and heard more "formal" music such as brass band music, military marching music, European classical music. They mixed this music up with African rhythms and country blues sounds using instruments such as clarinets, trombones and trumpets (often abandoned by the Civil War army bands). Jazz has developed and changed over and over again since those early days, into things like: swing; be-bop; free jazz; jazz funk and acid jazz. Some has even gone back to Africa and influenced certain types of African music all over again.

The jazz trumpeter, Louis Armstrong (1900–71) said:

If you have to ask what jazz is … you'll never know!

In other words, the music speaks for itself (like most music really!).

Gospel music Religious black American music. Slaves were "encouraged" to abandon African religions and to attend Christian churches and sing hymns. But they added their own unique African musical styles to the European hymn-singing. A stirring and extremely exciting new sort of music gradually developed and got its name in the 1920s. During the late 1950s some singers went on to perform a non-religious version of gospel – this became known as "soul".

City blues Some country blues musicians moved to cities like Chicago and began to use electrified, amplified instruments. Their music got a harsher, more urgent sound and many American and British rock and pop groups of the '60s, '70s and '80s copied this sound.

Rhythm and blues (R&B) A mixture of city blues music and jazz which got its name in the late 1940s.

It often has wailing saxophones and loud electric guitars. Singers sometimes sound wild and out of control (but aren't!) and occasionally shout words rather that singing them – it's very exhilarating to listen to. A more popular version of R&B became known as rock 'n' roll and changed pop music for all time!

The grandpop ... of pop!

"I love the blues, they hurt so nice."

One of the most chilling of the black American sounds to come out of the musical cooking-pot was the blues. Now you've read a bit about the early sorts of black American music you may be able to see why so many music experts think that the blues was the beginning of so much modern pop music such as rap, hip-hop, rock, soul, Tamla-motown, doo-wop, R&B and rock 'n' roll. These incredibly popular musical styles that grew from the blues have given masses of pleasure to millions of people but the grandpop (or grandmum?) of pop was born in circumstances that no one could describe as pleasurable.

101

The heartaching backbreaking birth of the blues: key notes

No one is exactly sure how the blues came into being, but this is generally what is thought to have happened...

- As the captive African people in America endured hour after hour of backbreaking work they sang their traditional songs in order to keep their spirits up.
- The years went by and the Africans began to hear other types of music ... and to learn the language of their masters (which was usually English).
- New generations of black Americans were born on the plantations and the traditional music of Africa eventually became a distant memory for many of them. The music they played and sang as they worked gradually changed from purely African music into a new kind of music that was partly European and partly African.
- The music continued to grow and develop long after the slaves were given their freedom. It eventually became known as the blues (though no one is really sure why it got that name).
- Even though black Americans were no longer forced to work as slaves after 1865, most continued to have a very tough time. Many white people treated them as less than human (especially in the southern states of America) and they had to put up with awful living and working conditions. They were often imprisoned or beaten for something as trivial as being on the street after 11 o'clock at night! It's hardly surprising that the blues grew up in very tough places, and was played by very tough people ... like James Baker.

Look out James Baker! – the oak's on you!

James Baker wasn't the only blues musician with a nickname. Lots of the guitar greats and boogie-woogie wizards of the past had their. There was : Cow Cow Davenport, Pine Top Smith, Bumble Bee Slim, Barbecue Bob and Ironing Board Sam.

Now who shall I be today?

The blues singer and guitarist, Blind Willie McTell (1898–1959) wasn't content with just *one* nickname – he had *seven* of them! He was also known as: Pig n Whistle Red, Hot Shot Willie, Blind Sammie, Red Hot Willie, Georgia Bill, Peg and Whistle Red and Barrelhouse Sammie. This must have caused problems for anyone introducing Willie/Sammie/Bill (?) at the music clubs where he made his 12-string guitar ring like a bell and sang his heartbreaking songs about lost girlfriends and bad luck. It certainly confused people who collected his records.

Something to do: form your own jug band and play some gut-bucket blues

What you will need:

● Plastic lemonade bottles in assorted sizes – these will be your "jugs" (a real jug band would have used empty whiskey bottles, but there'll be no need for that!). The bigger ones will give you the lower (bass) notes, the smaller ones will give the higher notes. The "jugs" should preferably be empty but they still work when they are part-filled (so why not swig as you gig?).

- A wicker waste-paper basket. This will be your "washboard" – unless your family still happen to use a real washboard ... in which case, borrow it! (Then tell them about the remarkable invention we call the washing machine!).

- Some thimbles. Put these on your fingers and scrape them on the basket to get that essential rasping, rhythmic, rat-a-tat-tat washboard sound. If you haven't got thimbles you can use something hard, like a key or a pencil to get the sort of sounds that really are well "wickered".

- A couple of well-gnawed bones – or spoons if the dog is still eating. Hold the spoons back-to-back in one hand like this: Now clack them once on your knee then once on the palm of your other hand. Repeat these actions until you get a rhythmic rattle and clatter going.

- A metre length of dowel, or some other sort of stick (such as an old broom handle), about a metre of string, a large(ish) cardboard box.

1. Firmly trap the dowel in one corner of the box under one of the flaps (which should be folded in).

2. Tie one end of the string to the top of the dowel and thread the other end through a hole at the top of the opposite corner of the box.

3. Tie a large knot in the end of the string to keep it in place. This is your "string bass". You pluck it to make a twanging, thudding sort of sound. You can vary the pitch of the notes by sliding the string to lengthen or shorten it as you play. **Important safety note** – put a wine cork or lump of plasticene on the end of the dowel to protect eyes.

- Some tissue paper and a comb. Wrap the tissue around the comb and hum into it to create the authentic kazoo sound (it should make you think of a

106

swarm of drunken wasps).

- Get the band together in a suitable venue like a garden shed, disused night-club (or your living room during the six o'clock news). This will be your jook joint. Your mission ... to get the joint jumping! But before you do you must all *practise*.

Every musician must practise and practise their instrument until it almost becomes part of them ... an extension of their soul?! (wow!), well, all right then – until they can get it to make a noise! Jazz musicians used to call their long, lonely practice sessions "woodshedding" – at one time in America you couldn't pass a woodshed without hearing lonely jazz musicians hooting and honking and wailing for all they were worth... and that was just the pianists!

To give themselves a few ideas and a bit of a "kick start" your musicians could try playing along with some blues records (your local library should have some CDs or tapes). Then, when you've all become fairly familiar with your instruments and the general "feel" of the blues, get together and work out some different rhythms. Once you've learned to play in time with each other, you can start to add some vocal sounds to your music!

General tip: many blues musicians let out their intense feelings by groaning, grunting, humming, howling and even shouting during their songs. If you want to hear some really first-rate moaning and groaning, try listening to "Smokestack Lightnin'" by

Howlin' Wolf (1910–76), then all have a good old groan yourselves.

Next step – make up a blues

The blues musician Son House (1902–88) said "…we made up our songs about things that was happening to us at the time and I think that's where the blues started." Blues musicians sang about things like their best mule dying, floods ruining the cotton crops and their sweethearts running off with their best friend. If your local cotton fields have recently been turned into a six-acre garden centre and you don't happen to have a mule that died recently you'll just have to make up a blues about something else, perhaps about the wretched life you have to endure at that cruel and unfeeling place called school, at the hands of those ruthless and brutal slave drivers known as teachers … maybe something like…

THE SPELLIN' TEST BLUES

WOKE UP THIS
MORNIN'
I GOT THOSE SPELLIN'
TEST BLUES
I AINT DONE MY
HOMEWORK
I KNOW I'M JUST
GONNA LOSE (MARKS)

BLIND LEMON SHERBERT

HOWLIN' GERBIL

OOWER! OOOWER!
HE'S GOT THE SPELLIN' TEST BLUES
THE SPELLIN' TEST BLUES!

BUS STOP

CLASS 4B

MY BEST FRIEND'S CALLED
BARRY
HIS SPELLIN'S REAL ACE
BUT WHEN I WALKED IN
THE CLASSROOM
HE JUST WEREN'T IN
HIS PLACE!

110

Your lead singer sings the main verses and everyone else repeats the choruses as they scrape and twang and stamp away in the background. This method of singing is known as a "call and response pattern". It was what the slaves and work farm prisoners did as they toiled in the fields. It probably gave them a feeling of togetherness at their bleakest moments and may have been a way of passing on messages. On the prison farms, as many as 300 prisoners would all be chained together and singing in this way – it was reported to be a really astonishing sight and sound!

Last bit – has your music "hit the spot"?

If you notice that the dog starts to tap its paw and wag its tail in time to the music you know that you are making some groovy sounds. Miles Davis (1926–91) the famous jazz trumpeter once said:

If a guy makes you tap your foot and if you feel it down your back you don't have to ask anybody if that's good music or not. You can always feel it.

New Orleans: music ... music ... music – from cradle to grave!

While the blues was growing up in the countryside of America another sort of music was developing in the towns and cities, especially in the large sea port known as New Orleans. This music was called jazz and in the early part of the 20th century New

111

Orleans was just full of it.

If you could "time travel" back to old New Orleans your ears would be in for a treat! You'd hear music everywhere – but not from CD players or radios! It would be coming from the mouths and guitars of blues musicians, the trumpets and trombones of jazz musicians such as Buddy Bolden (1877–1931) and Kid Ory (1886–1973), and the bands of jazz pianists such as Jelly Roll Morton (1890–1941). Jelly actually claimed to have invented jazz – but then again so did quite a few musicians. Jazz wasn't invented ... it just grew quite naturally. It was part of everyday life.

New Orleans had *live* music 24 hours a day, and you could hear lots of it for free! Music accompanied almost every bit of everyone's lives, from the cradle to the grave. It was played at christenings, at picnics in the countryside, on the steam boats on the Mississippi River, as an accompaniment to work, in restaurants and bars, at banquets and weddings, dances and street parades. And finally, when people died, they were given an extra-large helping of kicking, throbbing, pulsating music to send them on their way. New Orleans funerals really were something special!

Didn't he ramble ... didn't he gamble?

Black American funerals in New Orleans were very spectacular occasions. This is what happened:

1. Up to as many as five jazz bands would gather as the mourners prepared to follow the coffin to the cemetery. The names of the bands would be written on the sides of their enormous bass

drums and the brightly coloured sashes that the leaders wore. Many of the people present would be carrying rolled up umbrellas. The coffin was brought out and loaded on to a horse-drawn hearse and the walk to the graveyard (or "bone orchard" as it was known!) would begin.

2. The procession would be a really slow and mournful affair with jazz bands like the "Eureka" and the "Onward" playing sombre and solemn tunes and everyone feeling truly sorrowful. Just as you'd expect when people were playing their last respects to a dead person.

3. When the procession finally reached the cemetery, the bands would wait outside the gates while the burial ceremony took place. As soon as the coffin was in the grave and the last prayers had been said, the mourners would leave the cemetery and then ... everyone would go absolutely wild!

4. The jazz bands would strike up their jazziest, snazziest tunes, the umbrellas would be unfurled to reveal that they were decorated with vivid and flamboyant colours and in no time at all the mourners would be waving and whirling them in time to the music as they shimmied and strutted through the streets of New Orleans. Everyone would be singing and dancing while the bands played joyful tunes that were intended to celebrate the life of the dead person. They had lines like, "Oh didn't he ramble ... didn't he gamble ... 'til the good Lord cut him down!" which was a way of saying, "He really was a bit of a raver – wasn't he?" Bystanders, especially children, would join in with the celebrations. Some of them would even be playing their own instruments – this custom was known as "second lining". Many of the great New Orleans jazz musicians of the 20th century played in the "second line" when they were children.

Why did it happen?

This unusual way of conducting a funeral was probably related to the African origins of the mourners and musicians. In certain West African countries funerals are still held in a similar way today.

Last verse

If you played a modern jazz record to Buddy Bolden or Jelly Roll Morton and told them it was jazz, they'd probably be completely mystified and say,

No waaaay! We've never heard anything like ***that*** *in our lives.*

We've absolutely no idea what it is ... but it certainly ***ain't*** *jazz!*

Since those early days in New Orleans, jazz music has changed over and over again ... and so have all the other early forms of black American music that first popped out of the great American musical cooking pot. As they've all developed they've given birth to many of the sounds that are so popular today, like rock, soul, pop, hip-hop and rap. In other words, the mixing of musical styles didn't stop at the beginning of this century – it continued. It's still continuing ... not just in America but all over the world. And thanks to modern technology it's all a bit easier than it used to be.

Non-Stop Pop

One long pop and rock party

Since Elvis and Little Richard set thousands of teenagers reeling and rocking back in the 1950s, people haven't stopped partying to pop. In the last 40 years or so, dozens of styles of pop have come and gone, and thousands of performers have climbed up and down the charts. It would take a book as big as a mega-store and a chart the size of a dance floor to track their progress, so, if your favourite artist has been missed from this next dizzy dance through three-and-a-half decades of mind-blowing pop ... please don't blow your top.

Part One: The swinging sixties

During the early 1960s everyone went pop mad. It was reported that there were 10,000 pop groups in Britain at around this time, and they all wanted to be number one in the charts! Obviously, there wasn't room for them all to succeed but a very large number of them – like the Rolling Stones, the Kinks and The Who – did hit the big time! The results were amazing. Pop suddenly became so important that the adult world actually decided to reorganise itself to make room for this new music phenomenon. This is what happened:

● New "pirate" radio stations began broadcasting non-stop pop to music crazy teenagers. They weren't run by real pirates but by disc "jockeys".

RADIO CAROLINE

I'VE COME ABOUT THE JOB...

- Magazines were created so that fans could stare for hours on end at photographs of the stars and read fascinating articles about their shoe sizes, favourite breakfast cereals and interesting potty training experiences.

- Teenage "pop" fashions in clothing became big business. London became the fashion capital of the world.
- New big record stores began opening to sell the music that everyone wanted to hear – many of them are still around.
- New TV programmes were launched to show off the new groups that sprang up like mushrooms every week.

- Even BBC radio eventually woke up to the new music. They had the pirate radio stations closed down and started a pop channel of their own ... which they called Radio One.

117

From now on, instead of just being something that teenagers enjoyed in their spare time (as it had been in the early '50s), pop became a whole way of life. People listened to pop, they dressed pop, and they thought pop.

The Beatles – four bugs that caused a pop epidemic

Nineteen sixty-three was *the* year of Beatlemania in the UK. If you were a teenager at that time and had never heard of the Beatles it was probably because you were either: a) trapped inside a very thick balaclava helmet b) Cliff Richard's hamster, or c) attending a lost international Scout and Brownie jamboree in the Amazon rainforest (or all three).

Beatles timeline – how the Fab Four found fans, fame and fortune

- 1957 Liverpool: John Lennon (1940–80) meets 15-year-old Paul McCartney (b.1942) and asks him to join his skiffle group (a bit like a jug band – see page 98). The group is called The Quarrymen after John's old school, Quarry Bank Grammar.

- The band changes names, members (and underwear) quite a few times over the next few years.

- Liverpool is a good place to hear all sorts of music because sailors bring back lots of exciting new records from America that couldn't be bought in British shops. So, the band's musical heroes are rock 'n' rollers like Elvis Presley and Chuck Berry, and also blues musicians like Lightnin' Hopkins and Muddy Waters.
- 1962: They start calling themselves The Beatles – the name is inspired by Buddy Holly's old group The Crickets. They decide to approach a big record company to get first record released under their new name. But the audition in London doesn't work out too well...

SORRY BOYS - I HAPPEN TO KNOW THAT GROUPS WITH GUITARS ARE DEFINITELY ON THE WAY OUT.

DECCA RECORDS

Brian Epstein becomes their manager. Parlophone Records sign them up for their first recording contract. Their first single is, "Love Me Do", released October 1962. The band now consists of John Lennon, Paul McCartney, George Harrison (b.1943) and Ringo Starr (b.1940).
- 1963: Their next single, "Please Please Me" positively *smashes* into the charts at number one ... so does the next ... and the next! Other

Liverpool groups also become mega-popular – a new sound emerges, generally known as "Mersey-beat". "Beatlemania" begins in Britain.

How to recognise a Beatlemaniac

- Tendency to scream, cry, faint and riot when near Beatles.

- Usually rush around in huge crowd and "mob" Beatles (or anyone who happens to look like them) at every opportunity.

- Frequently bombard band with jelly babies at concerts – or send them through post (over fifty kilos delivered in one week in1963!).

- Often blasted with high-power water cannon by firefighters, grappled with by police in attempts to control them, seems to have no effect on them at all.

- Fill scrap books with Beatles' mementos including signed photos, concert tickets, jelly baby (said to have been sucked by a Beatle?!), one of Beatles' cigarette ends, twig taken from a Beatle's garden hedge, sock (George Harrison's), piece of toast taken from breakfast table (George Harrison's) …

- Older Beatlemaniacs think nothing of handing over huge sums of cash for Beatles souvenirs e.g. £27,000 for John Lennon's old leather jacket!

- 1964: The Beatles tour America and go on American TV – 73 million people watch! During the broadcast not one teenage crime takes place *anywhere* in USA! Beatlemania rampages around the rest of the world.

- 1966: The band gives up live performances after audiences become *so* noisy that the group can't hear themselves at their own concerts.

- 1967: They take six months to record the 40-minute LP *Sergeant Pepper's Lonely Hearts Club Band*. Many people think it is their best-ever record.
- 1970: Paul McCartney leaves group. The rest of Beatles decide to split up (perfect timing ... it's the end of the swinging Sixties, and the end of The Beatles!).

Four final flabbergasting facts about the Fab Four

- The Beatles have sold more records than any other group in the world ... ever! Their record company (EMI) estimates that over ONE BILLION Beatles tapes and records have been bought throughout the world.
- On 14 December 1963 the Beatles had *six* records in the UK top 20 ... all at the same time! They included LPs and EPs (that means extended play – or an LP that's having problems growing up) as well as the singles "She Loves You" (at number one) and "I Wanna Hold Your Hand" (at number two).

AND TONIGHT ON TOP OF THE POPS WE HAVE THE BEATLES, FOLLOWED BY THE BEATLES, THE BEATLES, THE BEATLES, AND THE BEATLES. BUT FIRST...ER... THE BEATLES!

- In 1964 the first five records in the American top 20 were *all* Beatles singles.

The Beatles' song "Yesterday" first appeared on their *Help* LP in 1965. By 1967 another 446 singers and bands had recorded their own versions of "Yesterday".

And they all lived hippily ever after?

The Beatles and quite a few other '60s pop and folk artists often sang about trying to make the world a better place. The words of songs like "All You Need Is Love" (Beatles, 1967) and "The Times They Are A-Changin" (Bob Dylan, 1964) had a big influence on teenagers. As a result, young people didn't rebel against their boring old parents by doing a bit of rocking and rolling (like they had done in the 1950s) – they used music to protest about all the squabbling and fighting that was going on in the world of adults (especially the war that America was fighting in Vietnam).

"We don't want to grow up to be a load of crabby, quarrelsome, rat bags like you lot!" they said to the grown-ups. "There's too much argy-bargy in the world. Let's have a bit of peace and love for a change. Us kids are all going to put flowers in our hair and freak out to groovy sounds and live hippily ever after … so there!"

Thousands of young people got together in parks and fields and went out of their way to be really pleasant to each other as they listened to stars like Bob Dylan, Jimi Hendrix, Love and the Rolling Stones at enormous pop festivals like Monterey (USA 1967), Woodstock (USA 1969), Hyde Park (UK 1969) and the Isle of Wight (UK 1969,1979).

These events were known as "be-ins". There were so many be-ins in 1967 that it became known as the

"summer of love". Many teenagers and some of the pop stars of the '60s were sincerely trying to use music to make the world a better place. Unfortunately, as the decade came to a close, one or two of the mega-stars began to forget their original ideas about how they might use music to improve society and got far more interested in other things ... like earning vast amounts of money ... and increasing their own sense of self importance.

The Seventies – a glimmer of glam followed by a plague of pulsating punk

The Beatles may have broken up when the 1970s arrived but by this time the non-stop pop party was positively powering ahead. Pop stars were enjoying enormous success – and many of them had begun to dress and behave as if they were permanently attending a party ... a fancy dress party that is! Their stage shows and clothes were so extravagant and flamboyant that fans turning up for pop concerts might well have thought they'd arrived at the local circus by mistake. But this was quite understandable, after all, Pete Townshend of The Who once said: "Pop music is ultimately a show, a circus..." This sort of "over-the-top pop" came to be known as glam rock.

A gaggle of glittering glam rockers

T. Rex (Marc Bolan) were once a '60s electric band but had to go back to acoustic (non-electric) music after a hire purchase company took their instruments back. They did hippy-type songs (about elves and pixies and things) with titles like "My People were Fair and had Sky in their Hair but now they're Content to Wear Stars on their Brows".

T.Rex later turned "glam", got a backing band with electric guitars (all paid for this time) and had big hits like "Hot Love" and "Get it on" (1971). Marc Bolan was killed in a car crash in 1977.

David Bowie (b. 1947) – in the late sixties, Bowie did flower power, hippy-type music (like Marc). He made an album called *Ziggy Stardust* and *Spiders from Mars* (1972) and performed as a glam rocker called Ziggy Stardust (he was supposed to be an alien who had become a rock star!). He dressed in a jump suit, platform boots and wore his hair red and spiky. Another LP from his glam period is *HunkyDory* (1971) which featured the hit single "Changes". It's now considered a "classic" album – in other words, it still sounds great after years!

John Lennon said of Bowie's music, "It's great ... but it's just rock 'n' roll with lipstick on."

DAD! THERE'S A SPIDER FROM MARS IN THE BATH!

Slade Started off as a skinhead band but later became glam rockers. Their music was loud and repetitive, and sounded almost like chanting football fans. Some people thought all their songs sounded the same but teenagers loved them. Their song titles were often misspelt e.g. "Look Wot You Dun" and

"Cum On Feel The Noize". One MP was so worried about this that he mentioned it in Parliament – he was afraid it would have terrible effect on young people's spelling ability (wot du yu fink reeder?).

WE WERE MEANT TO BE CALLED 'SLIDE' – BUT WE COULDN'T SPELL IT

Ten staggeringly simple steps to becoming glam . . .

. . . with tips from glam star Gary Glitter (a shining example to all wannabe glam rockers).

1. Get some "platform" shoes with soles and heels that are so incredibly high they give you dizzy spells every time you wear them!

2. Team your "platforms" with flared trousers and shirts decorated with enough sequins and spangles to sink a showboat.
    Alternatively wear a suit made entirely from silver paper (like

Gary did) – but expect to be referred to as the "Baco Foil kid" (like Gary was).

3. Stuff your shirt with shoulder pads the size of small sofas.

4. Arrange your hair in a "bouffant quiff" so enormous and menacing that it causes dogs and little children to run away and hide in cupboards.

5. Wear lots of make-up (especially if you are David Bowie or Marc Bolan).

6. Give yourself a name that goes with your new image. Gary tried Terry Tinsel and Stanley Sparkle before he came up with Glitter!

7. Make records with lots of loud drums and bass, catchy melodies and words that are instantly memorable and tons of fun to sing along with (like Gary did).

8. Have a string of 11 consecutive top ten hits (like Gary).

9. Sell a million copies (like Gary did with "I Love You Love Me Love").

10. Live a very extravagant lifestyle ... perhaps in a country mansion complete with a heated out-door swimming pool, automatic bedside champagne dispenser and £6,000 pounds worth of remote controlled "motorized" curtains (like Gary did). But beware – your extravagant and self-indulgent lifestyle may eventually cause you to run out of money (like Gary did!).

So take care of your dosh ... and watch out for those punks!

Ear-piercing Music

By the mid-'70s quite a lot of people were feeling a bit disillusioned with glam rock. Nothing fresh, exciting or original seemed to be happening on the music scene and the highly paid glam stars all seemed to be smug and self-satisfied with the rather stale and boring music they were producing. In addition to this, unemployment in the UK amongst teenagers was on the increase and quite a lot of young people were feeling pretty fed up with the world in general. Conditions were perfect for the new music revolution known as "punk rock" ... and the creation of the angry, anti-social, all-swearing, all-aggro, "all or nothing" group known as the Sex Pistols...

Ten things you definitely shouldn't know about punk rock and the Sex Pistols

1. Punk began in New York, USA, where it was played by groups like Patti Smith, the Ramones and the New York Dolls. The music was "fast and furious", filled with feeling, fire and frenzy, with the words sometimes shouted rather than sung.

2. And this is what Punks were like . . .

3. Malcolm McLaren, the manager of the New York Dolls, spotted Johnny Rotten (real name, John Lydon) when he was hanging around a shop he

owned in London. McLaren got him to sing along to a record on the shop's jukebox, thought he looked good and turned him and his pals into a punk band called the Sex Pistols.

4. In 1976, a television presenter called Bill Grundy invited the Sex Pistols on to his show. He didn't think much of the band and dared them to say something "outrageous" live on air – so they did. But it was Bill who got into trouble. The next day the story got headline treatment in the newspapers … he got the sack!

5. The Sex Pistols signed a £40,000 record deal with the EMI record label who promptly sacked them for bad behaviour just a few weeks later – but let them keep the money!

6. The following month they signed a new record deal for £150,000 with A&M records at a ceremony outside Buckingham Palace – just *one week* later they got the *sack*! This time they were allowed to keep half of the money (perhaps they should have been called the "Sacked" Pistols?)

7. A few months later, the Sex Pistols signed yet another record deal with Virgin Records. There was trouble again – this time the workers at the factory where their "God Save the Queen" single was being produced, refused to have anything to do with the record and threatened to go on strike because the cover featured a picture of Queen Elizabeth II with a safety pin in her nose (apparently, she only ever wears that sort of thing in the privacy of her own home).

8. The strike was narrowly avoided and the record was released (it was the year of the Queen's

Jubilee, 1977). Many shops refused to stock it and the BBC banned it from TV and radio (but this didn't stop the Duke of Edinburgh secretly pogo-ing to his copy).

9. The group fired Glen Matlock, their bass player, because he could play his instrument too well (so they say!) He was replaced by Sid Vicious, whose musical ability was less obvious (or completely non-existent).

10. The Sex Pistols were banned from almost everywhere in the UK, so they went on tour under a false name: the "Spots" (**S**ex **P**istols **O**n **T**our!).

Mark E. Smith of The Fall (a punk rock group from Manchester) said, "Rock and roll isn't even music. It's a mistreating of instruments to get feelings over."

If you want to make yourself a name in pop ... first make yourself a name!

Gary Glitter and Johnny Rotten aren't the only popsters who've given themselves new identities. Quite a few musicians conveniently forget their real names and give themselves fresh ones like ... Slash, Iggy, Sting, Bono and Dozy! Having a new name really does seem to be part of creating a completely cool new pop image for yourself.

- Plain old ex-English teacher, Mr Gordon Sumner (b. 1951), doesn't sound like he'll take the world of pop by storm, does he? But someone called "Sting" just has to be the bee's knees!

- If you're about to set out on a record-breaking musical mega-tour the last thing you want to be called is Reg Dwight! With a name like that people are going to be asking you to service their central heating boiler or sell them a kilo of wet fish, rather than to drive them potty with your sensational singing and piano playing. Far better to call yourself Elton John (b. 1947).

- If you want to sell lots of records and you've got a name like Yorgos Kyriakou Panayiouto, you've definitely got a good reason to ditch it. It doesn't exactly trip off the tongue does it?

You'd be surprised at just how many well-known musicians are hiding behind false names. See how many you identify.

1. David Jones 2. M. Ciccone 3. Fanny Mae Bullock
4. Marvin Lee Aday 5. William Perks 6. Harry Webb
7. Declan McManus 8. Eric P. Clapp 9. F. Bulsara
a) Cliff Richard b) Elvis Costello c) Meatloaf d) Bill Wyman (of the Rolling Stones) e) Madonna f) Eric Clapton g) Freddie Mercury (of Queen) h) Tina Turner i) David Bowie

Answers – 1i, 2e, 3h, 4c, 5d, 6a, 7b, 8f, 9g

So now you know – they made their names up. Their parents weren't that cruel after all!

AND I NOW NAME THIS BABY... MEATLOAF?

The earbending Eighties

The '80s got off to a bad start when John Lennon was murdered (aged 40) in New York by a man who had asked him for his autograph only a few hours earlier. Not long after this, quite a few pop stars began hiring permanent bodyguards...

Meanwhile, back at the recording studios, a new set of up-and-coming popsters were putting together a completely fresh sound and look for the new decade. These musicians were known as the New Romantics and their elaborate appearance and poetic, rather "dreamy" style of music was said to be a reaction to the harsh, ugly and raw sound of punk.

A razzle of romantics – followed by a moment of madness

Spandau Ballet: were school friends who formed a band in the 1970s. They made "glossy", electronic, pop songs and were the first New Romantics to get in top 40 with "To Cut a Long Story Short" (1980). They wore frilly shirts, big scarves and kilts (no bagpipes though ... phew!).

134

Duran Duran: the lead singer Simon Le Bon made "smooth" catchy songs with lots of synthesizers. The group members had elaborate haircuts (e.g. two-tone wedge), and wore eye make-up and silk scarves. They had big hits with "Rio" and "Hungry Like The Wolf" (1982).

ABC: were influenced by punk, disco and new wave of late '70s. The lead singer Martin Fry has an attractive, high "yearning" sort of voice. The songs had clever lyrics, good melodies and were highly polished (not rough and crude like punk). Their album *Lexicon of Love* (1982) was described by music critics as "early '80s pop at its best" (so give it a listen!).

Not all pop fans in the early '80s spent their days swanning around in silk shirts and sighing sorrowfully to the synthesisers of the New Romantics. Quite a few were quite happy to jerk, jig and sing along to the feel-good "chug-a-lug" beat of...

Madness: were not in the slightest bit New Romantic. They were more like everyone's favourite, totally barmy uncles, all performing together in one band. They made music in a catchy jamaican "ska" style with a shuffling, insistent "a chic-a-chic chic" rhythm. They took their name from a song by ska music hero Prince Buster. Their lyrics are full of humour, and often about growing up in '70s London e.g. "House of Fun" and "Baggy Trousers" (1980). They dressed in sharp suits, sunglasses, "pork pie" hats and danced around jerkily as they sang and played. And they're still singing and playing! "Madstock" reunion concerts are now held regularly (so what are you waiting for?).

Some pop stars are more mad than Madness themselves...

Forget all your troubles – go to Neverland!
Michael Jackson was one of the most successful musicians of the '80s. His album *Thriller* is the biggest-selling pop album of all time, (over 40 million copies sold). As well as being famous for his music Michael is also well known for his eccentric behaviour and lifestyle. He has been able to use the vast earnings from his music to make some of his wildest dreams come true. Which of the following fantastic stories about him are said to be true ... and which are false?

1. Michael used to sleep in an oxygen chamber so that he would remain young-looking for as long as possible. True/False

2. Michael's ranch, Neverland, contains a private zoo with 200 animals, fairground rides, a mock Indian village and a two-storey video arcade. True/False

3. Michael's skin has gradually become lighter and lighter over the years. He admits to having had two plastic surgery operations but blames his changing skin colour on an inherited skin disease. True /False

4. Michael sometimes dresses in girls' clothes and travels under the assumed name of Janet. Many people mistakenly believe that he has actually got a sister of this name. True/False

5. A former member of Michael's staff said that Michael never had breakfast without first putting on full stage make-up. True/False

6. Michael's nose isn't actually his own. It used to belong to Tiny Hamstrong of the Chicago R&B band, Blacksnake. True/False

7. Michael leapt on to the stage and began hitting Jarvis Cocker of Pulp when Jarvis was performing a pop version of "The Farmers in his Den" with some ten-year-old children at the Britpop music awards ceremony in 1996. True/False

8. Michael is very keen on Disneyland. On one visit to the theme park he wore a surgical face mask and was pushed around in a wheelchair. True/False

9. Michael once offered Pete Townshend of the British pop group, The Who, $50,000 for his ears. True/False

10. Michael has a pet chimpanzee called Bubbles. He and Bubbles have little tea parties, spend hours

playing together in Michael's den and have 20 different matching outfits. True/False

Answers: 1. True; 2. True; 3. True; 4. False; 5. True; 6. False; 7. False – It was actually Jarvis who leapt on the stage as Michael was performing a song. Michael was dressed as Jesus. Jarvis thought this was all a bit over-the-top, so he wiggled his bottom at the audience – and was escorted off the stage. 8; True; 9. False; 10; True.

Just like Mozart, Michael made an early start on his career in music. At the age of nine he became the lead singer in the Jackson Five, the Tamla Motown, "soul and rhythm" group that he sang in with his four brothers.

His solo career began in 1972 when he had a hit with "Got to be there". By the time he was 14 he had made such a success of his pop career that he had become a millionaire (and was finally able to give up his paper round). Since then he's been wowing a world-wide army of fans with his vital videos, dynamic dancing and mesmerising mix of pop and soul music styles.

Something to do: How to become an international pop and rock mega-sensation – overnight!

Now that you know so much about music you'll no doubt be desperate to form a pop group of your own and achieve fame and fortune for yourself? Here's how to do it!

What you will need:

- Some charisma. If you aren't sure whether you've got this or not, answer this simple question: do large crowds of people gather around you in the playground or street for no apparent reason? If they do, you've got charisma, so put on your shades and prepare to be famous.

- A "roadie" (road manager). This is the person who drives you about when you are on tour, lugs your sound equipment and instruments to gigs, sets them up and checks that they are working properly and, most importantly of all, says "One ... Two ... One ... Two ..." into the microphone before you come on stage. Get your dad to be your roadie – but remember ... from now on he must wear his hair in a ponytail, and change his name to Deek, Squiffo or Nogger!

to Deek, Squiffo or Nogger!

- A press agent. Your press agent will constantly pester music mags to review your latest singles and gigs, tell them of your forthcoming plans, and offer to fly music journalists to review your appearances abroad. When you become mega-famous the journalists will get their own back by pestering your press agent.

- A manager (or agent). Your manager/agent will organize your gigs, record deals etc. and, more importantly, give you your pocket money. Get your Aunty Elsie to be your press agent *and* manager – but first she must change her name to Candida, Laetitia or Zariana, get rid of her specs and dye her hair green.

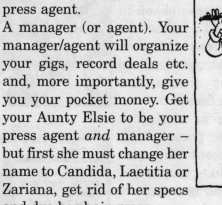

Now you can get on with being famous!

7.00 a.m. Get out of bed, put sunglasses on, clean teeth, muss up hair and, if you are a boy, do *not* shave!

7.15 a.m. Practise chord sequences (and sneering) on air guitar (imaginary guitar, often played by drunken grown-ups at parties).

7.25 a.m. Ring friends, tell them to muss up hair because they are now your *group*, all must turn up at your house for 9 a.m. press conference … sunglasses, big shirts and sneering compulsory from now on at all times!

MESSY HAIR

SUN GLASSES

BIG SHIRT

SNEER

9.00 a.m. Have press conference with Aunty Elsie.

9.01 a.m. Decide on name for group, the more noticeable the better. Short ones seem to have been the most popular recently so why not something like Plop, Blot or Splot? If it doesn't feel quite right, don't worry you can always change it when the group breaks up (then reforms) next Friday.

11.45 a.m. Name sorted? Now get some instruments – if you can't afford the real thing use the ones you've made in the "Something to do" sections. Tennis racquets, frying pans etc. will make good guitar substitutes until you can afford proper ones (fans probably won't notice – just keep the lights low at gigs).

Handy tip: Don't worry if you can't play your instruments too well (or at all). True pop musicians have never let the inability to play music get in the

141

way of success. Just remember what Sid Vicious of the Sex Pistols once said when he was asked about his guitar technique: "You just pick a chord ... go twang ... and you've got music!"

12.30 p.m. Twanging practice for whole group.

1.00 p.m. More sneering practice.

1.20 p.m. Hang around "with-it" places looking cool e.g. trendy restaurants/ bistros in West End of London (or outside local chip shop).

1.25 p.m. Sign thousands of autographs (...for each other).

2.00 p.m. Go to studio (your bedroom). Make up songs. Keep them simple. Noel of Oasis once described their songs as "...just silly little nursery rhymes..." so this shouldn't be too much of a problem.

3.00 p.m. Sign record deal (with each other). Make tape of songs, duplicate lots of copies on twin-deck cassette player.

3.30 p.m. Go to record shops – sell tapes to them.

3.45 p.m. Go to record shops – buy tapes back again. Why? So sales rocket and shoot your single up charts of course! Once song is in top 30 DJs will give it "air time" (play it on radio) and everyone will rush out to buy it and you'll get your money back in no time!

4 p.m. Have huge row with rest of band after accidentally clobbering drummer with tennis racquet during extra-wild guitar solo. Get Aunty Elsie ... sorry, Zariana ... to phone music papers like NME, Melody Maker etc. to give news of band's imminent break up. Good idea to give them a ready-made headline, something snappy like "Bat Splat Splits Splot!" Get little sisters and brothers of band members to gather round front gate sobbing and wailing and begging you to stay together (promise to give them 10p afterwards).

4.10 p.m. Crisis over: all friends again. Do reunion gig in local park.

4.20 p.m. Aunty Elsie to issue press release and circulate rumour of forthcoming world mega-tour. All band put on big coats and dark glasses and go to local airport ... railway station ... bus stop – rush around for a bit.

4.40 p.m. Go home.

5.00 p.m. Get news of adverse reaction to growing fame. Quickly sort it by telling mum that she'll just have to contact your agent for appointment to discuss controversial "untidy bedroom incident"!

5.30 p.m. Band now internationally famous. Local child (your cousin) and lost Japanese tourist mill about outside front gate for at least half a minute.

5.45 p.m. Stay cool! Handle fame. Close all the curtains. Watch telly for rest of evening.

8.59 p.m. Amazing news! Tape has finally gone platinum (serves you right for leaving it on top of hot radiator!).

The Nineties

In the early '90s the charts were dominated by American music and dance music that relied on an insistent beat, simple and repetitive lyrics, flashing lights (and not much else in quite a few cases). Some people (in the UK) began to look back at the swinging '60s and think of them as the "good old days" of pop when groups sang proper songs with words that actually meant something and tunes that went round and round in your head for days after you'd heard them. Quite a few music fans and critics were of the opinion that British pop music was in a poor state of health and might not last out the decade.

Then, just when it looked as if pop's terrible tiredness was totally terminal, along came a whole new set of bands like Blur, Suede, Pulp and Oasis who all made songs that had humour and ideas and words of more than one syllable in them ... and tunes that were whistleable, and singable, and hummable ... and Britpop was born!

144

Three helpings of Britpop followed by an oodle of Oasis

Pulp: was formed in 1981 when Jarvis Cocker, the lead singer was still at school. He said he formed a band

> *so that girls would like me, because I had glasses and bad teeth and wasn't any good at sports.*

Their first gig was performed in the school dining hall!

His'n'Hers album was released in 1994 – and at last "Pulpmania" began. There's a sort of frantic, urgent feel to Pulp songs which often tell stories about relationships with girls. Newspaper critics have described Pulp as: "rooted firmly in '70s tack and '80s electronic disco"; "every song an exquisite melodrama".

Blur: were said to have "spearheaded" the Britpop scene. They were once referred to as "the best British band since The Beatles. In 1993 the *NME* said Blur's music was "instantly catchy and full of melodic twists". The album *Modern Life is Rubbish*

(1993) – was described as having a "classic English sound with roots in the Kinks". In 1994, their album *Parklife* – sold two million copies world-wide.

SO WHY DID YOU CALL YOURSELVES "BLUR"?

Suede: appeared on the cover of *Melody Maker before* they'd even released a record. They were the first '90s band to "chart" with lyrics (song words) that said something (rather than just being nonsense rhymes). In 1992 *The Observer* newspaper said "while their lyrics are provocative (challenging and controversial) musically, Suede are relatively traditional – their sound is old fashioned with a distinct glam rock aura." Their album *Suede* (1993) was described as having appeal for "insensitive slobs" as well as "soulful types".

SOULFUL TYPE

COR! THEY'RE BRILL!

SING SING

INSENSITIVE SLOB

Pop pickers get lost in musical desert then find ... Oasis!

Every now and then, experts declare that pop music is dead for ever. And then, just as they're saying "Oh it's all over now, there'll never be another band like

The Beatles or the Rolling Stones or REM, guess what happens? Along comes another exciting and talented new band … like Oasis.

oasis fact file

- **Members:** Noel Gallagher (b. 1967) – guitar/vocals/writes all the songs; Liam Gallagher (b. 1972) – vocals – often referred to as "our kid', by Noel; (b. 1966) – Paul "Bonehead" Arthurs (b. 1972) – rhythm guitar; Paul "Guigs" McGuigan (b. 1971) – bass; Alan White drums

- **Home town:** Manchester
- **Favourite football team:** Manchester City
- **Origin of name:** Named after venue where The Beatles played their first-ever Manchester gig
- **Record company:** Creation Records
- **First single:** "Supersonic"
- **First LP:** *Definitely Maybe*
- **Second LP:** *What's The Story (Morning Glory?)*
- **Third LP:** *Be Here Now*
- **Biggest gigs:** Played outdoor gigs at Knebworth and Loch Lomond in 1996. Attended by nearly a third of a million fans. Tickets completely sold out in nine hours.

- **Other claim to fame:** Liam and Noel Gallagher are notorious for falling out with each other. At the end of 1996 one music magazine said that Oasis had begun the year as a band and ended it as a soap opera!
- **Future career:** Some music critics have predicted that Oasis will eventually be as big as the Beatles ... what do you think?

POP THE QUESTION! ARE YOUR TEACHERS TOTALLY TRENDY? HOW WELL DO THEY KNOW THEIR OASIS?

1. OASIS played their first gig at the Boardwalk club in Manchester in 1991. Noel hadn't yet joined the band but he was in the audience. What did he say when he saw the band performing?

a) It's the worst gig I've ever seen
b) Flippin' eck, our kid's wearing me best trainers!
c) This band is brill...I can't wait to tell our kid about them.

HA! EASY PEASY!

2 Oasis were discovered by CREATION RECORDS when they were playing at a club called KING TUT'S on 31 May 1993. The club had told them they weren't booked but they played anyway. What had they threatened to do if they weren't allowed to play?

a) Scream and scream until they were sick
b) Tell their Mams
c) Burn the club down
d) Release their collection of Pet Tarantulas

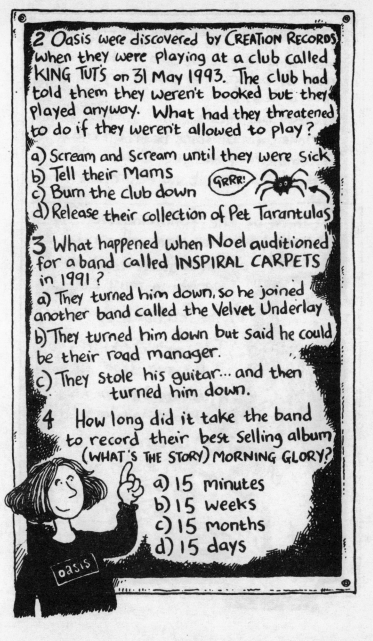

GRRR!

3 What happened when Noel auditioned for a band called INSPIRAL CARPETS in 1991?

a) They turned him down, so he joined another band called the Velvet Underlay

b) They turned him down but said he could be their road manager.

c) They stole his guitar... and then turned him down.

4 How long did it take the band to record their best selling album (WHAT'S THE STORY) MORNING GLORY?

a) 15 minutes
b) 15 weeks
c) 15 months
d) 15 days

oasis

5 What did Oasis insist that the managing director of Creation Records must do before they would sign a record deal?

a) clean his teeth
b) Make them all some beans on toast.
c) Remove his Manchester United shirt.
d) Beat the whole band at arm-wrestling

6 Which of the following were Noel's favourite three album's of 1996?

a) Manic Street Preachers- Everything must Go
b) The 3rd Beatles Anthology
c) Tibetan Nose Flutes A-Goo-Goo
d) What's the Story Morning Glory?
e) Ocean Colour Scene Moseley Shoals

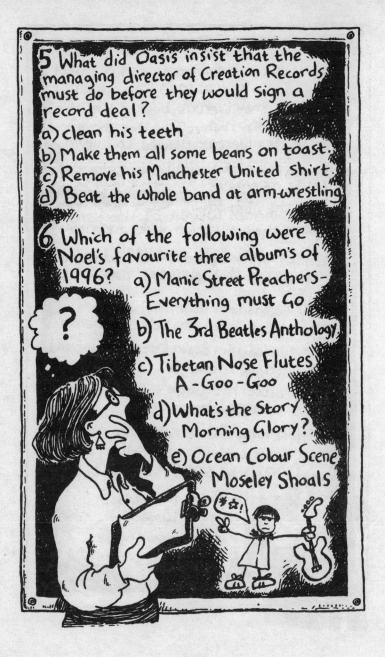

7 In 1995 the band played the two 'biggest ever' indoor gigs in Europe at Earl's Court in London. What else was remarkable about these events?

a) The enormous crowds quickly used up the air in the concert hall and the show had to be delayed while replacement supplies of oxygen were helicoptered in.

b) The combined weight of the fans jumping up and down caused Earl's Court to sink 10 centimetres.

c) The music was so loud that earth tremors (mini earthquakes) were reported in neighbouring areas of Kensington and Chelsea.

8 At the signing of the recording contract with Creation Records in 1993 Noel demanded that he should receive a special reward when Oasis eventually hit the big-time. What did he ask for?

a) Singing lessons

b) A chocolate brown Rolls Royce

c) An expenses-paid weekend for five in Manchester.

d) A lifetime's supply of Smarties.

e) Some Money

Answers: 1a Noel offered his songwriting and musicianship skills to the band on the condition that he had complete "artistic" control over them – they said "Yes!"; 2c; 3b Noel became the "guitar technician" to the Inspiral Carpets, went on tour with them in America, studied their approach to pop and decided he "could do it better"; 4d; 5c; 6 a, b, e Noel idolized the Beatles and said he wished he "could have written all of John Lennon's songs"; 7c; 8b; Noel eventually got his chocolate-coloured vintage Rolls Royce car. He was given it for Christmas 1995 by the boss of Creation Records. When he saw it he said, "Well, what am I going to do with it? I can't drive!"

It's refreshing, isn't it, the way pop music can keep renewing and recreating itself – and it's usually just when the old stars are getting a bit stale and are just about past their "thrill by" date. New people ... new ideas ... new music = new listening enjoyment for millions!

Last verse

Remember what the record company executive said to The Beatles when he gave them the cold shoulder? "Guitar groups are on the way out." He must have left his crystal ball at home that day. Talent spotting obviously wasn't his strong point. Then again, perhaps the whole thing was a bit of a mix-up and he actually meant to say guitar groups are **"Way out!"** as a sort of compliment? Ever since the early 1960s the charts have been full of nothing but guitar groups (almost!) – and it's mostly because

152

of The Beatles. In just the same way as they were inspired by Elvis and Chuck Berry, their incredible success went on to inspire further generations of young music addicts to pick up guitars and have a bash at becoming the next Beatles. Some groups, like Oasis, have actually come quite close to it but none have ever actually equalled or overtaken the fantastic success of The Beatles yet. But who knows? There may well be some music-mad under-15s plucking away at their guitars at this very moment (or reading this book) who are set to become the super groups who will make the mind-blowing music of the 21st century? Let's hope so!

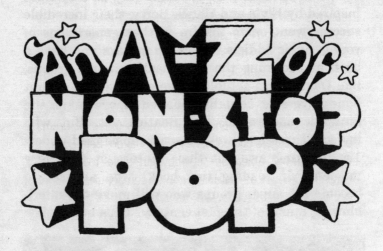

An A-Z of NON-STOP POP

The following alphabet is a sort of whistle-stop, non-stop bop around "Planet Pop". It'll just give you a taste of some of the stunning pop sounds you could try. If you fancy sampling some of them, all you have to do is rush out to your local music megastore and treat yourself to six or seven sack loads of CDs or a couple of crates of cassettes, then get listening!

On the other hand, if you're still paying off the bank loan on your gold-plated C.D. player, you could just pop along to your local record library and borrow some of the music they've got there. Most libraries charge a small fee for loans and have a reasonable selection of all sorts of music – but make sure you return the loans in good time ... even if you have fallen in love with them.

Finally, if you don't fancy parting with any money at all, you could just do what a lot of grown-ups do, and make friends with someone who has an absolutely enormous record collection!

A – A. O. R. Adult Oriented Rock (sort of thing ex-punk teachers, some mums and dads listen to). Sometimes called MOR ("Middle of the Road") music e.g. Phil Collins; Sting; Sheryl Crow; Dire Straits.

B – Bhangra British Asian pop music developed from Asian folk dance music in which wooden barrel drum was beaten with heavy stick. Now uses lots more instruments including guitars, saxophones and tablas (pairs of drums played with fingers and palms) e.g. Bally Sagoo; Safri Boys.

C – Country American "cowboy/girl"-style folk music. Originally known as "hill-billy" now mega-popular all over world. Musicians voices and guitars very "twangy" e.g. Dolly Parton; Emmylou Harris; Nanci Griffiths; Willie Nelson.

D – Disco Began in '70s. Rhythmic and sometimes mesmerizing dance music played in discothèques e.g. Village People; Earth, Wind and Fire.

E – Electronic Uses lots of modern high-tech instruments like synthesizers to create "space age" sounds that you just can't get from other instruments (musicians have morbid fear of power cuts). Also called "techno" e.g. Orbital; The Orb; Kraftwerk.

F – Folk Ordinary people's music – started long ago all over the world. Sometimes has a rustic, or country, flavour to it but also protests about injustice. Modern version with electric guitars called folk rock e.g. Fairport Convention; Bob Dylan; Joan Baez.

G – Garage Home-made rough-and-ready sort of pop often recorded in … garages! (listen out for tell tale squeak of up-and-over doors!) e.g. The Seeds; The Nazz.

H – Hip hop Black music of early '80s often played out of doors on portable stereos and danced to by energetic, acrobatic "break" dancers. developed into Rap e.g. De la Soul; Public Enemy; Fugees.

I – Indie (short for independent) Pop that is not part of main pop industry (if it can help it). More concerned with making original and satisfying music than earning billions of bucks. If successful, small indie shrimps can get swallowed up by huge hungry record company sharks e.g. The Charlatans; The Wedding Present.

J – Jungle A bit like rap but with a "fuller" sound from more instruments. Words sung rather than being shouted, spoken or chanted (as in rap) e.g. Goldie, Springheel Jack..

K – Kraut rock What pop fans (and Kraut rock musicians) call German version of "progressive rock" – big sound, lots of organs, big guitar chords e.g. Tangerine Dream; Can.

L – Lo-fi Simple (but potentially powerful) pop recorded without aid of a squillion studios full of sophisticated recording equipment. More about feeling and enthusiasm than slickness and technique (possibly recorded in garage?) e.g. Sebadoh; Eric's Trip.

M – Metal Started in '60s with white R&B groups like Led Zeppelin but became much louder and more aggressive by '70s. Also known as Heavy Metal or Thrash Metal. New listeners advised to wear at least three sets of earplugs e.g. Guns 'n' Roses; Meatloaf; Iron Maiden.

N – New Wave Fresh, tuneful, lively pop that followed on from punk revolution. More melodious, carefully thought out and definitely less exhausting to listen to than punk e.g. Blondie; Elvis Costello; Talking Heads.

O – Old Grey Whistle Test What pop composers did when they had just written a new song – played it to the *old, grey*-haired doorman at recording studios. If he could whistle it after one listen they knew it would be a hit (also name of '70s TV rock show).

P – Progressive rock Linked to glam rock in '70s. Attempt to develop pop away from simple individual songs into big themed "concept" creation albums (almost like a classical symphony) e.g. Pink Floyd; Yes; Deep Purple.

R – Reggae – Jamaican music that developed from ska. Very insistent, regular and rhythmic bass beat. Often played through gi-normous speakers, know as "sound systems". e.g. Bob Marley and the Wailers; Big Youth; Toots and the Maytals

S – Soul – Began as non-religious version of Gospel, with blues feeling mixed in (see page 97). Lots of emotion, frequently backed by big, brassy band sound. Singers and instruments often seem to be sobbing and moaning. More rhythmic version developed into Tamla Motown. e.g. Sam Cooke; Aretha Franklin; Otis Redding.

T – Teeny-bop Pop enjoyed by younger fans – incredibly popular and successful despite what older listeners say. Sometimes unkindly described as "drip pop" e.g. Spice Girls; Take That; Boyzone.

U – Underground Non-mainstream pop music often with

"cult" following. Quite a few pop trends (like punk) start off as underground but eventually pop up into daylight and become mega-popular e.g. Velvet Underground; Big Star.

V – Video Used to increase sales of new pop releases. First used successfully by Queen in 1975 to promote sales of "Bohemian Rhapsody"

W – World Pop from other cultures such as that described in X, Y, & Z...

X – Xhosa-Traditional South African pop of 1950s often mixed with American jazz styles e.g. Woody and the Woodpeckers.

Y – Yo pop Pulsating pop from Nigeria (West Africa) described as being "full of thunder and lightning" e.g. Segun Adewale.

Z – Zydeco African-American pop music from swamp country of Louisiana (with French "Cajun" influence). Pounding relentless beat uses accordions, guitars and enormous corrugated metal breast plate which musicians strap to chest then pound and scrape for all they are worth e.g. Beau Jocque; Clifton Chenier.